Gift of the Hit
COLLECTED STORIES - VOLUME 1
Life Happens, Then You Get to Choose

Peter M. Davison
with
Joscelyn Duffy

Tellwell Talent
www.tellwell.ca

ISBN
978-1-77302-171-3 (Ebook)
978-1-77302-170-6 (Paperback)

Table of Contents

LIFE HAPPENS,
THEN YOU GET TO CHOOSE.

"Between stimulus and response, there is a space.

In that space is our power to choose our response.

In our response lies our growth and our freedom."

— Viktor E. Frankl, Concentration Camp Survivor
and Author "Man's Search for Meaning"

Dedication

It is very humbling as I look back and chart the way the universe works to congeal compilation works like this. Books like this don't just magically appear; they are result of an integrated and connected web of life. My heart is beaming from ear to ear for all people who supported this project. Firstly, it would not have been possible without the inspired sharing of the contributing authors. To all of you, I am humbled by your collective wisdom, and overwhelmed with gratitude for the unique journey each of you took to bring your stories within these covers. Thanks to those who recommended the contributors, and for everyone's ongoing patience and belief in the project. How you came to be part of the project would make a fascinating read about the power of manifestation and serendipity.

I raise a glass in celebration of the projects phenomenal ghostwriter and co-author, Joscelyn Duffy. She is a relentless stalwart in the face of her own health challenges, maintaining an unshakable faith. She continued to believe when I felt discouraged and overwhelmed by the obstacles I encountered between balancing everyday life with the demands of a learning curve in my first self-publishing adventure. Her signature sums up her life's passion and she fulfils exquisitely: *Helping others find and fearlessly express their authentic voice.* Thanks for being our literary midwife for the brain child we now have the pleasure to cradle in our hands.

To the spiritual teacher who was integral in my perspective shift years ago, Chris Walker, thank you. He supported the awakening of my consciousness of the magnificent laws of nature at work in our lives every day. He challenged that lopsided perception, when something is only seen as all good (infatuated) *or* all bad (resented), can create suffering/dis-ease from our attachment to a polarized opinion that is contrary to nature's law of balance.

Most of all, thank you to my patient and devoted wife Andrea for understanding all the late nights and to my awesome kids, Hannah and Vance, for their forgiveness for me sneaking away from family movie time because I had another idea to write down.

Preface

When I ran into an old friend I hadn't seen in years, we had but a few seconds to catch up on our news. I shared, somewhat proudly, that I had gotten married at age forty-eight, became a father of two at fifty-two and was diagnosed with Parkinson's disease. Which one of the three captured my friend's focus? She picked up on the fact that I had an incurable degenerative disease, expressing how sorry she was about my diagnosis.

I suggested that she need not to feel bad, because my diagnosis was actually the best thing that had ever happened to me. She stared at me in disbelief. Feeling compelled to clarify, I blurted out a concise explanation that surprised even me: "Because of my diagnosis, I surrendered to love."

That single thought was the entire essence of my life's struggle captured in one sentence.

What began with my personal memoire, *Gift of the Hit*, quickly grew into a series of books, beginning with this one, *Gift of the Hit: Collected Stories - Volume One*. Collected Stories was born as I began to share with others about the path through my hit, to love. What occurred was magical: others immediately wanted to share their stories with me. The exchange of our truths, real pain and incredible triumphs led to a bond of deep understanding, empathy and compassion between us.

It is my hope that the stories within these pages do the same for you, helping you realize that you are not alone in your challenge to find meaning in and embrace the greatest hits of your life. In reading the words of these incredible contributors, may you discover a new sense of self-love and love for others, knowing that our hits happen in all different shapes, sizes and seasons. Some take years to work through. What matters is that we embrace where we are and continue to recognize that we always have the strength to find our way through the tumultuous times.

J.K. Rowling said, *"Destiny is a name often given in retrospect to choices that had dramatic consequences."*

What if that which we judge as good or bad is merely a construction of our mind, and every judgment is a coalescence of the lifetime of interpreting our experience? This book introduces a potentially controversial, yet irresistible, concept that may shake up the way you think about life. It is one that supports that in every experience, there may be at least two sides, two points of view, two perspectives, two possibilities…or perhaps even more multiple facets discovered through deep exploration. What these authors have embraced are no small feats. They have faced stillbirth, organ transplants, cancer, mental health, ALS, Parkinson's, anorexia, being burned, a heart attack, sexual abuse, a severe car accident, a stroke, blindness, becoming widowed, autism, testicular cancer, lupus, ADD, divorce and Alzheimer's. However, each contributing author is much more than a convenient label.

Every one of this book's contributors have, like me, discovered love and something bigger. That force has guided them through the hardest times in their lives, to a place where light shines through the dark, and hope overrules despair. The stories in the *Gift of the Hit* collection showcase the strength of the human spirit through the accounts of ordinary people who have overcome extraordinary events – those who have chosen to find the gift within their hit.

It is my wish for all of you that you are able to find your way to a place of embracing what is and allowing yourself to be witness to, and grateful of, the gifts that unfold from there.

Life happens, then you get to choose. What will your choices be?

Contributed Gifts

Tatiana Morren Fraser

HIT:

Shattered by the unbearable pain of losing her son Andrew and enduring his stillbirth, Tatiana was left wondering how to resume her life when it had been torn apart.

GIFT:

Allowing her son's spirit to guide her, Tatiana found the courage to feel the rawness of her grief, comprehend the impermanence of life, and heal in a way that opened her to a personal rebirth and another son.

A Focus on Love and Life
– TATIANA AND DAVE

In 2010, my husband Dave and I were happily enjoying our very full life our a one-year-old, Lachlan. He is a joy, adding more love, fun, and energy to our lives than we had ever thought possible. In January of that year, we were surprised to learn that we were going to have another baby in October. Our initial reaction was one of complete shock. We had not planned this! With Lachlan being just a year old, the two babies would be quite close in age. However, I realized that I had very much wanted another baby, and I was thrilled. I was filled with a beautiful happy sense of calm, along with anticipation for my new life with two active children.

The pregnancy proceeded without incident. I felt great throughout, aside from the usual morning sickness during the first few months. In fact, it was a far more reassuring pregnancy than my first, in which I had suffered from high blood pressure and needed much medical attention. I felt wonderful up to the end of the pregnancy. I even took the last month off work, to ensure that I was not subjecting the baby to any unnecessary stress or anxiety. I can remember being so focused on what life would be like after the baby was born. I planned for the meals that I would make in advance, so that we had healthy dishes prepared during the initial stages after his birth. As I imagined what our lives would be like with two children, I felt nothing but joyous anticipation for this wonderful addition to our family.

The day of our baby's birth, I was experiencing fairly regular contractions, spaced far apart. I knew that we would probably need to head to the hospital at some point in the day. Since my labor was clearly at a very early stage, Dave decided to go to work. My mum had travelled from Ontario to be with me, so she and I spent a lovely day together. I even had a nap that afternoon. When I woke up from my rest, I recall feeling extremely cranky, and my belly was very tight and hard. I thought it was probably the contractions. We went to pick up Lachlan from daycare and Dave at work. Once we got home, my contractions started getting more frequent, and we knew labor was starting. We were very excited!

After getting Lachlan settled in for the night, I managed the contractions for a few hours, and then asked our doula to come. At this point, I started wondering if I should be feeling the baby move more frequently, so I called the IWK Children's Hospital information line and spoke to a nurse in the delivery unit. I wasn't overly worried. When the nurse discovered that this was my second baby, she indicated that if I was worried at all, I should come in for an assessment. As soon as I hung up, I felt the baby give a big kick and move around, so I was reassured. We decided to continue with our planned home birth.

Our doula arrived shortly after, and for the next several hours, we concentrated on managing my pain. At one point, we noticed that my water must have broken and there was meconium in the fluid. We headed to the hospital right away, as that was certainly concern. Once we got to the hospital, we were still sure that everything was fine, and we would be heading home the next day with a beautiful new baby. When the nurses discovered a fair bit of meconium in my fluid, they took me in to check the fetal heartbeat right away. My attending nurse was clearly trying to remain calm, but I could tell that she could not find the heartbeat. The on-call obstetrician came in with an ultrasound machine, and the room was very quiet while she and the nurse examined the screen.

I remember looking at the wall, and noticing that our doula, who was holding my hand, had her head down on the bed and was praying. At this point I knew without a doubt that the baby had died. Although I was doing my best to keep my head turned towards the wall, the obstetrician forced me to turn my head so that she could look into my eyes, and said words that will remain etched into my heart: "Tatiana, I'm sorry, but there is no heartbeat."

At that point, I felt like something had snapped inside me and that I was cut-off from all my feelings. It was as though I was floating outside and above what was happening. I recall feeling angry, and saying: "*Fine*. That's just *fine*. What do you propose to do now?" The obstetrician was very kind and firm, and let us know that the best thing at this point was to let labor continue, and to deliver the baby naturally.

We were taken to a delivery room, where we were assigned a wonderful, experienced nurse who had helped women to deliver stillborn babies. She truly knew what she was doing. The entire floor of the nursing unit was there to support us. All the obstetrical staff came into our room to introduce themselves, and let us know that they were there to help us as best they could. My husband and I were in complete shock. I think we were numb. I got an epidural immediately – something I had planned to avoid if possible, but given the situation I knew I couldn't face the pain of contractions on top of everything else.

After several hours of remaining emotionally numb, and experiencing no progression in labor, I realized that my body was probably listening to the directions from my brain to tighten up and close down. Dave and I talked about how important it was to us to deliver the baby naturally, and we realized that if I continued to not progress, I would need to have a c section. We decided that we were going to have to face up to what was happening. It was excruciating to let the feelings of pain enter our bodies. However, once we let ourselves feel the pain of our loss, we also were able to also feel our love for our baby. We quickly realized that our love had not changed one iota, and that a parent's love for a child cannot be changed by whether the child is alive or dead. With that perspective, we realized that our baby's birth was still our baby's birth, and we could bring him into the world with joy and love. In fact, we realized this was the only thing that we *could* do for him, and we recognized how much we wanted to do it.

After we went through the beginning of our healing process, my body began to open up, and labor progressed, until it was time to push. I recall our doctor coming in to begin helping with the delivery, and giving me an encouraging talk about how natural birth is the best option in a still-birth situation. I still remember the irritation I felt. I told her that she didn't need to give me a pep talk. "I am *so* excited to deliver my baby. I'm good!!" I said.

The feeling of my body doing what it was designed to do was absolutely incredible. I remember noticing that the room was filled with an almost tangible love and support, as though everyone was focused on something that was far bigger than any of us. In fact, I almost sensed the air was shimmering with a white light glowing throughout.

When baby Andrew was born, Dave cut the umbilical cord as we had planned, and immediately we both held and cuddled him. He was perfect and beautiful. It was the most bittersweet moment I have ever experienced. I felt as though my body had accomplished something truly miraculous in helping this baby come into the world, and yet, I was devastated at the fact that he was dead. I could only think of all the things we would not get to do with him. I was acutely aware that these moments in the hospital were the only moments we would ever have with him in his physical form. It was as though we needed to compress a lifetime together into a few hours. We dressed Andrew in one of the sleepers we had brought with us, and were able to take as many pictures as we wanted. We now have so many beautiful pictures of Andrew, for which we are profoundly grateful. My sister and mother were able to come to the hospital and spend some time with Andrew, cuddling him and taking pictures.

Eventually, we noticed that he was beginning to change physically. It was an extremely difficult decision, but we decided to ask the nurse to take him. I learned afterwards that we probably could have asked to keep him with us overnight, but we were given the impression that we should give him back to the nurse when we were ready. Watching the nurse walk away with our baby, knowing that we would never see his body ever again, was too much to process. I think we both began to go numb again. The only thing I could feel was an overwhelming sense of exhaustion.

We were able to stay overnight in the hospital and when we were ready, we headed home the next day. It felt as though we were re-entering our lives in a chapter that we had not planned, and for which we had no blueprint. How could we resume our lives when we felt like they had been torn apart? We felt as though our lives had been put on parallel trajectories – in one trajectory we had a beautiful, healthy second baby boy, while in the other trajectory we had lost him and were slowly figuring out how to reconstruct our lives around that reality. For a while, it felt as though both trajectories were happening at the same time. I wondered if I actually might be going crazy.

For the first week or so, I felt like I was on automatic pilot. I would get up to take care of my two-year-old and get him to daycare, and then collapse back in bed and stare at the wall. Sleep was impossible. 'Near sleep' was the worst, as all the memories and feelings would come flooding back. For the most part, I felt like I was in the most excruciating pain imaginable, and I did not know how to cope with the overwhelming emotional sting. Having real, physical pain to cope with (from the effects of the birth) was almost a relief.

Dave and I were lucky to have an immense amount of support. My father flew out to Halifax immediately, joining my mother, sister, and Dave's parents. Our entire family was with us to support us, help look after Lachlan, do the cooking and housework, and let us focus on healing. We also had wonderful support from our doula and a colleague of hers. Both women were enormously available, and in their own ways, they gave us resources, ideas, and emotional support to help us through the worst of the first several weeks.

We also participated in a group support session at the hospital for families who had experienced infant loss. That group was a lifeline for us. Once a week, we spent a few hours with other couples who had lived through experiences similar to ours. The group was led by a very knowledgeable, sympathetic, and wise chaplain from the IWK. It was through that group that we were first able to begin to face the reality of what had happened, and get our heads around how to put the pieces of our lives back together. We realized that we needed and wanted to heal in a healthy way, so that we could continue to parent our older son.

We received very helpful advice about the grieving and healing process in those sessions. We learned to respect each other's grieving needs. That meant that if Dave needed to mow the lawn five times a day, I understood that it was part of his process, and not a way to avoid thinking about Andrew. Similarly, Dave accepted that if I needed to talk excessively to process my feelings, that was how I was working through my grief.

We also found that we needed breaks from the pain. Frankly, there is a limit to how much emotional pain the human body can endure. Although we felt odd about it, we took 'grief breaks' by watching silly television shows. It was as though we could temporarily dissociate ourselves from the grief, knowing that it would be there once we were ready to go back.

I also learned a lot from some excellent resources online and books by authors who had either experienced infant loss or psychologists with expertise in the grieving process. I realized that I needed to take time to process my grief and work through the loss. I took six months off work, and structured my life so that my full-time job was to heal. I would take my son to daycare twice a week, and on those days, I sat in a special space and worked through various exercises to help process my experience. It was the hardest job I have ever had. I had to force myself to do it. It was agonizing, but soon, it began to feel good to take the dedicated time to do this work. Afterwards those sessions, I would feel like another part of my grief had loosened, like a little bit of pointy, sharp, pain had become more slightly dulled. However, I never, ever, felt as though my goal was to remove the pain; it was to figure out how to live with it.

I also was determined that if I could, I would find something in this tragedy that would make our lives better, and make me a better person. I wanted Andrew's legacy, and his impression upon our lives, to become something much more than pain. I felt as though we owed it to him to ensure that his death would also be a gift to us – to help us learn how to live our lives in a more meaningful, authentic way.

I found my journey through the grieving process to be an immensely spiritual one. Before Andrew's birth, spirituality had not played a particularly large role in my life. Dave had always gone to church, and believed in God, but it had not been a prominent part of our relationship. My experience during Andrew's birth, of feeling profoundly that some spiritual force, larger than anyone in the room, was present and supporting everyone present, has never left me.

I found that it helped me to use a practical workbook. My doula recommended a book called *Mending Invisible Wings* – a workbook designed for women who have experienced infant loss. It uses a creative approach to expressing feelings and working through the various stages of grieving. It does not shy away from facing the most difficult parts of this kind of loss head on. Dave and I also found that having a professional psychologist to talk to was very helpful. It ensured that we continued to respect each other's unique process for dealing with the loss and working through the grieving process. We did not expect each other to process grief the same way, and allowed one another space when we needed it, and were there to support each other when we needed that. Our psychologist was also very helpful for me, to help me decide when I was ready to go back to work, and how to do that in a healthy way. Dave had gone back to work a few weeks after Andrew's birth, and that was what he needed to do. I wasn't ready until six months later.

As I worked through the healing process, I began to be more appreciative of things in my life, and I realized that I could choose how to perceive a situation. For example, instead of feeling frustrated with my two-year-old when he delayed us getting out of the house, I decided to see my time with him as precious. I choose to manage the situation so that we built more time into each step and we could enjoy it, rather than rushing through it.

The time I spent at home with Lachlan during this period was immensely precious to me. He was aware that something significant had happened, but of course, he did not really understand it. I was able to spend several days a week with him – an experience I never would have had, except in this unique situation. The beauty of the experience was, however, tinged with the sharp sadness of the shadow of the baby whom I thought would be doing all those things with us. As time went on, I began to be able to enjoy the time with Lachlan in and of itself, without thinking of the baby who wasn't there. Eventually, I was able to feel joy in moments, to laugh, and have fun. They began to happen sporadically, and over time, they happened more frequently.

It took a very long time to feel 'normal' again. Years even. As we worked through our grief, the feelings of joy, love, and happiness outweighed the feelings of sadness and distance. Eventually, we decided that we were ready to make the decision to try to have another baby, and with that decision – and the subsequent birth of our son Nathaniel – we healed even further.

We will always feel the pain of Andrew's birth. Never will we be able to go back to the time before we experienced this loss. It has changed us profoundly. We will always worry about our children. We will now always see our children as gifts from God, never taking their presence for granted. For me, it is a constant struggle to manage my anxiety about my children's safety and well-being. I am aware that if I let the fear take over, I would constantly be imagining all the horrible things that might happen to them. At the same time, I think we are more aware of the need to let go of the things that do not matter, and focus on only the truly important things in our lives. Raising our children to be compassionate, loving, people is far more important to us than whether they are at the top of their class in school, or the best swimmers in their swim class.

The biggest lesson that we have learned from our experience is that we have the ability to choose our attitude and our perspective. We can let circumstances dictate our feelings and attitude, or we can choose how we want to view things, and shape our circumstances into the life we want to lead. For us, the choice is to be healthy and focus on love and life as we move forward together.

About Tatiana

BIO:

Tatiana is a very busy mother of two wonderful, active, boys and two step-daughters. She lives in Bedford, Nova Scotia with her husband, Dave, and their children. Originally growing up in Kingston, Ontario, she is now proud to call Nova Scotia her new home. She and her family love living close to the ocean, and enjoy all kinds of active, outdoor activities around the province. Their favorite summer activities include camping, exploring new places, and meeting new people. Tatiana also works with the Province of Nova Scotia, and is passionate about helping to develop public policy that positively impacts the province and the region. She welcomes any questions about her experience, through emails sent through www.giftofthehit.com.

Tatiana and Dave with their sons Laughlin and Nathaniel

Halina St. James

HIT:

In a matter of seconds, Halina lost the power of speech and the ability to write. What would it mean for her life, and her career as a speaker and communications coach?

GIFT:

As she worked to recover from the stroke, Halina took a hard look at what was really important in her life. She realized her priorities had to change if she was to avoid the pressure and stress that caused her illness. She calls her stroke a stroke of good luck, because it gave her a second chance.

A Stroke of Good Luck

– HALINA ST. JAMES

On December 27, 2012, my husband Neil, my mother and I had just finished breakfast. My mother had spent Christmas with us and we were about to drive her home. At breakfast, I read her a letter that I had received from Poland a couple of weeks before Christmas. I had been wondering when to discuss the upsetting contents with my mother. The letter was about my step-father, who had died ten months earlier.

My step-father was Polish, and the letter was from his sister, whom we had never met. The sister claimed we owed her $50,000 from my father's estate. That was a bit of a shock. I shared the contents of the letter with my husband, but I didn't tell my mother about it right away. I didn't want it to spoil Christmas.

When I finally read the letter to my mother on December 27th, I thought she would get upset and create a scene. She didn't. She just said she didn't know anything about any money. We, she said, would have to do some research. That was code for "Halina, you have to investigate this." I sighed – another thing on my already loaded plate. I had just dealt with my step-father's death, funeral and the emotional nightmare faced when his ashes were impounded by bureaucrats in Poland, I had nursed my mother through lung cancer surgery and navigated the sale of her house in Ontario and her move to Nova Scotia. Oh, and I run my own business as well. On the bright side, I was grateful there had not been the big emotional scene I was dreading when I read the letter to my mother.

After breakfast, I went upstairs to change my clothes so we could drive my mother home. I felt fine. I took off my clothes and stood in front of my double closet, trying to figure out what to wear. Normally it would take me about one minute to decide on my wardrobe, but I couldn't move. I was transfixed by all the clothes. After a while, I started to slowly walk along the closet. I started to finger and linger over pairs of pants and sweaters. I did so for a good ten minutes. I just couldn't make a decision. I was touching the clothes, but in a distant, disembodied sort of way.

Disembodied is a good way of describing how I felt: it was as if a part of me was looking down, watching myself touching the clothes, touching the clothes, touching the clothes. I was aware of what I was doing. I knew it was bizarre. I also knew I typically have no problem picking out what to wear. This time, I just couldn't decide. This was the start of my stroke.

My stroke targeted my left brain. That's your analytic, logical, systematic side. My left brain was screaming "something's wrong, something's wrong," but my right brain – the expressive and creative side that sees the big picture – kicked in and overrode the left brain. The right brain produced a surreal sense of well-being. The left brain was warning of trouble, while my right brain was singing "Everything is beautiful, in its own way." The two hemispheres of my brain were at war with each other. I was having a stroke…and I couldn't care less. Everything was beautiful. It was like being in a trance. I was aware, but not concerned about anything. I continued fingering and lingering over my clothes.

Finally, I said to myself, "Halina, picking an outfit is not that difficult. Get a grip girl." With great effort, I got dressed. I went to the bathroom to put on some lipstick. I was still in my happy place, courtesy of my right brain.

The left hemisphere of your brain controls the right side of your body. I'm right-handed. My right hand picked up the tube of lipstick. So far so good. But then, like in a dream, my hand drew a pair of lips on my right cheek. I had no control over it. Wait a minute, I thought. That's not right. I wiped the stray lips from my cheek. Then I watched, fascinated, as my right hand, my devil of a hand, picked up another lipstick and drew a second pair of lips on my cheek.

I had wiped the second set of stray lips off my cheek and was standing in the dressing room when my husband came upstairs and found me. He asked if I was okay. I said yes. Truth be told, if he'd said my hair was on fire I would have said yes. 'Yes' was the only word I could say, only I didn't realize it yet. Neil knew something was not right. He asked if I wanted to rest while he drove my mother home. I said yes.

When Neil returned home, I was lying on the bed. I wanted to tell him to cancel an appointment with our chiropractor for later in the day. When I went to speak, all I could say was "yahmm, yahmm, yahmm…." I was frustrated. I had totally lost my ability to speak, just like that. I could think, I just couldn't speak…apart from saying "yahmm."

Neil, thinking he was being helpful, gave me a pen and paper. That's when realized I couldn't write. I just scratched a jumble of words. I could not control my right hand.

We called 911. I went to the hospital. While we waited in the hospital corridor in emergency, the paramedic with me pointed to a clock on a wall and asked me what it was. I said, "Yahmm". He then said, "That's a clock on the wall." I said, "That's a clock on the wall." We looked at each other. This was the first time I said something other than 'yahmm'. The paramedic then said, "Peter Piper picked a peck of pickled pepper." I repeated, "Peter Piper picked a peck of pickled pepper." Then he asked me what Peter Piper had picked. I said "Yahmm." I could repeat a phrase, but I couldn't answer a question. Eventually I saw the doctors. I had tests. I had scans. I had x-rays.

On December 27, 2012, I had a stroke, and it was the best thing that ever happened to me. I was not a typical candidate for a stroke, or at least I didn't think I was. At sixty-five years of age, I exercised, watched my diet and wasn't obese, let alone overweight. And yet I had a stroke. Why?

My neurosurgeon said my stroke 'exquisitely' targeted the speech center of my left brain. Generally, most stokes fan out and affect more of the brain. Many people have paralysis or other lasting physical problems. Because my stroke was so targeted, the only effect was to prevent me expressing original thoughts, reading or writing.

I'd taken my hit. I was admitted to hospital. Perhaps it was because my brain had short-circuited, or perhaps it was the meds I was on, but I was strangely serene. So serene, indeed, that I didn't blink when I was put in a ward with three men. I like my privacy, and at any other time I suspect I would have been asking for a private room in a quiet part of the ward. My husband teases me that we can't stay in a hotel without having to move rooms at least once, and yet, there I was in a room with three men, and only thin blue curtains to guard our privacy and dignity.

"I need to pee" was my introduction to one of my companions. He had a leg encased in plaster after getting airborne and crashing heavily while sledding with his son. (His son, clearly more safety conscious than his dad, was unhurt). Across the room, another companion was also encased in plaster. He looked as though he'd been frozen in time while trying to call a waiter or a cab. His right arm was plastered and suspended from a pulley above his head. "The cat did it," he said when I asked what had happened. The family cat had hopped into bed with him, inadvertently sinking a claw into an already infected finger on his right hand, sending poison coursing through his body. Apparently the elevated arm slowed the progress of the poison in the right arm, while the antidote was pumped into the left arm.

The story of the cat attack was a wonderful bonding moment between the three of us: three very different characters, with very different reasons for being in hospital. We found ourselves supporting and encouraging each other towards recovery. The biggest life lesson for me, however, was a comment from the third man in the room. He was older and lived in a rural part of the province. For some time, he had been struggling with a neurological condition that had caused his right eyelid to lock in the closed position. But that wasn't why he was in hospital. He was there because the condition had now closed his left eye. There was nothing wrong with his eyes, he just couldn't open his eyelids in the way most people can.

When I wandered over to say hello to him, he used his left forefinger to raise his left eyelid so he could see me. I couldn't imagine being plunged into darkness because I could no longer keep my eyelids open. When I asked him how he was coping, he amazed me with his response.

"It's nothing that can't be borne," he said, peeping at me from under an eyelid propped open with a finger. I wondered if I would have anything like his grace and fortitude in similar circumstances. Once again, I found myself getting a gift from a hit. This time, my ah-ha moment had come from this complete stranger's response to his adversity.

In terms of my stroke, I have no doubt that I was very lucky. Overnight, my speech started to return. Words came back haltingly at first, but I can tell you reassuring it was a relief to be able to express any thoughts, no matter how slowly and uncertainly the words as they returned to my tongue. I had to re-learn my alphabet. I sat on the hospital bed, singing my ABCs like a small child. I was pretty good until O and P, but Q and R and the letters that followed gave me a lot of trouble. I didn't use S, so there were no plurals in my emails.

In hospital and during my recovery, I kept a journal. It's a very graphic illustration of how the stroke devastated my ability to write. The first few pages are spidery and full of frustrated crossings-out. Gradually the crossings-out are fewer and fewer. This sixty-five-year-old was quite pleased with herself when she started to join the letters together.

The doctors still don't know what caused my stroke. Maybe we never will. Here's what I think caused my stoke: stress, stress, stress – all the stresses of dealing with aging and ailing parents. It was all the stresses that build up on every one of us, which we too often shrug off.

I believe my stroke was a combination of stress, and of me not paying attention to what was happening in my life. The last five years had been especially stressful… and I thought I was superwoman. I thought I could handle it all. I could just keep on going, like the Duracell bunny.

Does this sound familiar? Do you think you can do it all? I suspect that a lot of you do? Nothing's going to happen to you. You're not going to have a stoke, or heart attack, or cancer. You are not going to die. You are immortal. Right? You can handle everything that's thrown in your path. Right? After all, that's what you've been doing for as long as you can remember. That was the way I used to think. I could handle it all: disgruntled relatives, three aging parents, growing a business, focusing on my husband, and dealing with clients. The only person I didn't pay attention to was myself.

One of the airline safety rules about oxygen masks is that you always put your mask on first, then you help someone else. Good rule. Because I thought I was superwoman, I never put my oxygen mask on first. I was ready to help anyone and everyone, no matter how challenging… and even if I ran out of air myself.

Suddenly, because of my stroke, I was aware of other people having strokes. Many were younger than me. They had more money, more power and they were probably just as busy. And yet, they had a stroke. A stroke doesn't care who you are.

We get up in the morning to our perfectly planned lives. We have our schedules and our routines. We don't plan to have a stroke, or a heart attack. Yet if we don't take care of ourselves, in a blink of an eye, all of our plans mean nothing. As a good friend told me when I had my stroke, I got tapped on the shoulder. The message was to change – change the way you live, change the way you deal with stress, and change your attitude to life… or next time you might not be so lucky. And so, I changed, because I realized our time on this earth is so fleeting. I didn't want to waste a second of it.

The first thing I did was book all the vacations I wanted to take in the next twelve months. I planned five great trips. I booked my business and clients around my vacations. In the past, I used to book my work first and plan my life around it. Now, I'm booking my life first and planning my work around my life. I decided to have fun, not only during vacations, but every day. I chose to put the oxygen mask on myself first, before I help anyone else.

Next, I promised myself if something stressful like that letter from Poland came along, I was going to deal with it right away. It was crazy for me not to. You put something off because you think you're protecting someone. Even if you are, at what cost to yourself are you doing so?

I also decided that I am going to say 'I love you' more often to my husband, my mother and everyone I care about.

With every choice, I started doing reality checks. Is X really important? Will my life be better or worse if I do X? I am making smarter choices with everything in my life. And if I make mistakes, I make a real effort to stop stressing about them, to stop replaying them over and over in my mind, and to stop having that proverbial pity party. I choose to look at why a mistake happened and what it really is teaching me.

I spent most of the year after the stroke focusing on myself. I decided to look realistically at what was stressing me out, and do something about it. I was determined to rid myself of my ancient stressors – some of which were unresolved issues from my childhood. I worked with a variety of healers. I saw a physiotherapist and got a weekly exercise routine. I had a yoga therapist come to my home and teach me restorative yoga. I worked with an energy healer. I saw a naturopath and adjusted my vitamins and minerals to complement the medications I was on. I continued working with my chiropractor and my massage therapist, and I continue seeing my psychiatrist. I also started meditating more – something I had done only sporadically in the years before my stoke.

Every day, I continued to work on the part my brain that was damaged during the stoke. I continued to sing my ABCs. I wrote cursively in my diary. I read out loud. I played mind-challenging games on my computer. Slowly, I recovered.

Writing about my stroke has been therapeutic. It has provided me with a record that I read over and over again, to remind myself of all the things I need to do to live a healthy, smart, stress-free life each day. Today, I feel I am ninety-nine percent of the way back to where I was before my stroke. My stroke was a big wake up call. It helped me realize just how much we are stressed out, and how our lives develop an insane momentum which is difficult to stop. We don't truly look at our lives objectively as a whole, in order to see what's really going on with ourselves. When we don't stop and consider what's really happening in our lives, we begin to think everything is so important. Everything needs our attention. We can't let go. And yet, it is the act of letting go and surrendering to the moment, that will give us the greatest fulfilment.

I am grateful for my stoke. It was my stroke of good luck. It made me change. It made me live in the moment. I really think it saved my life, by making me realize what is really important. It made me realize that I am my own responsibility. If I want to live a long, healthy life, I have to just do it. I am responsible for what I do, how I do it, and when I do it. I am responsible for all the choices I make.

Am I perfect? Absolutely not. I live one day at a time. Some days are good. Some not so good. But I now take responsibility for each day. I understand it's not having everything that seemingly matters in life; it's about appreciating what I do have. And what I do have is me. If I take care of me, then everything will be beautiful.

About Halina

BIO:

Halina St James had already had a rich and varied life by the time she received the gift of her hit. She was born in a Displaced Persons in Germany at the end of World War 2. Her Polish parents joined the flood of migrants looking for a new life in Canada. Halina tried acting and nursing, before embarking on a career as a producer for the CBC. Halina was travelling with NDP leader Ed Broadbent when their small plane crashed in Northern Quebec. Fortunately, everyone walked away unhurt. An assignment to cover the first Gulf War in the Middle East led to her meeting and marrying a BBC TV producer. After a spell in London, England, they settled in Nova Scotia. Halina started *Podium Media & Communications Coaching* to help people improve their public speaking and presentation skills. Besides coaching, Halina speaks about the lessons she learned from her stroke.

Website: www.podiumcoaching.com

Halina St. James

Paul R. Roy

HIT:

After job losses, the surrender of businesses that he had proudly grown, and the end of his marriage, Paul wondered if he could triumph over an ongoing struggle with ADD and an endless pursuit of wanting to be somebody in this life.

GIFT:

Paul came to embrace the relentless energy, drive and determination of his ADD as the fuel to propel him to a life of great abundance as a successful businessman and compassionate coach for fellow entrepreneurs.

The Blessings of ADD: A Story of Perseverance
– PAUL R. ROY

When you're young, you don't really worry about *who* you are. Life is simply a series of opportunities to get out and actively play and enjoy… and in my case, very actively so. I was born the third of four children and grew up in a happy and lively family. My father was a humble world-renown cardiologist. My mother was the daughter of a successful businessman and friends with all the right people. Very early on, I learned to be a part of all the right clubs in our upscale neighborhood. We were part of a sailing community, and I was afforded the opportunity to become a competitive skier. As I stood looking over the metaphorical fence of life from the comfort of our home, my eyes were wide with child-like wonder and I could only imagine my life growing bigger and better from there on in.

In many ways, I couldn't wait to grow up so that I too could be *successful*. While we, as children, grew up with the luxury of financial abundance within our family, the money was not ours to have. We had to find jobs and earn our own. And jobs I did find! At ten years of age, I positioned myself as the neighborhood guy for hire. I mowed lawns and shoveled snow. I had a wood working business run out of our basement. Without conscious awareness, I became an entrepreneur very early on in life, and quickly discovered that I was passionate about work. I also loved the feeling of having cash in my pocket. Granted, I enjoyed spending my earnings as much as making them, so I had an incentive to keep making more.

I attacked everything I did with full gusto. To only partially exert or complete seemed like a waste of time. With the exception of school, I excelled in whatever I did.

The belief in our family was that if you wanted to go to university, you had to (financially) find your own way there. All of my siblings graduated from university. I didn't even go. While I had discovered my obvious proficiencies, being a student was not one of them. I was deemed to have *concentration problems*. Studies were an area in which my concentration levels created a big problem. School bored me. I scraped through, but always with grades in the lower half of the class. Every now and then, a fantastic teacher would provide hope and support, helping to launch me to the top of the class. For my entire childhood life, I rode the educational seesaw.

Back in the 1950s and 60s, the terms ADD or ADHD didn't exist. My excessive energy and inability to fully focus gained me the classification of being *hyperactive*. A normal day for me consisted of expending my excessive energy through sports, until I was called in to do my homework. Retaining anything from a book felt like a misguided effort for me. As soon as I read a paragraph, a word or thought would tweak a memory and I would be cast away into a daydream. Television had the same effect. I wanted to get to the end point of the show. Everything in the middle was just *fluff*. My parents were exasperated and didn't what to do about my being *hyperactive*, other than to send me off for a barrage of mental tests. I spent hours being questioned by a psychiatrist – an experience that I most definitely did not broadcast around the schoolyard.

The multitude of tests that became the norm in my life revealed one telling point: I may have spent much time at the bottom half of the class in grades, but by no stretch of the imagination was I dumb. My IQ was 128 – a score that would put me in the top four percent of the population. Capture my interest and I would remember every word. Bore me and I was a lost cause for retention.

So how does a young man termed as *hyperactive*, living with ADD, survive in the school environment? Well, you don't actually. I flunked grade ten because I decided to spend the year at the pool hall. My dad knew all along, but he never said a word. He knew the best medicine was for me to fail. I hated school so much that I didn't even attend graduation … once I finally made it there.

After high school, most of my friends went on to university. I went directly into what I loved: more work. I was determined to be a business owner, just like my successful grandfather. The plan was to use work as a means of gaining first-hand knowledge to become an entrepreneur. I had big dreams of being a success – a *somebody* – equipped with the fancy sports car and all. And so began my obsession with becoming a wealthy businessman.

I worked as a bill collector for a collection agency and a roadman for a finance company. I got customers to pay their bills, as I solved my own lust for money. I met the love of my young life, got married, bought a big house and a business, and had two sons. Everything in my life seemed to be set magically in motion, on direct course for victory. There was no life too big in my vision of success. Our home was the place where other kids loved to come to play. We went on family sailing trips and ski vacations, and I did my best to go out and earn more to keep up with the demands of our lavish life. I felt like Superman.

I was the guy who others saw as going out at lunch for a hamburger and coming back with a brand new car. That was, until the Free Trade Agreement was embraced in Canada and the rules of business changed; allowing the U.S. retailers to walk right in and scoop up our customers. Things quickly went to hell in a hand basket. The coupling of the *American invasion*, my thirst for the big life, and the recession led to the collapse of our family business, and an abrupt end to my goal of having a net worth of a million dollars by the age of thirty-five. I managed to get to $800,000 before it all came crashing down. In four short years I was over $200,000 in the hole and bankrupt.

Crumbling down with my business was my self-esteem. I felt as if I had shamed our family name, and myself. There I was, front-page news in the local paper – a former president of the business district whose failures were broadcast for everyone to see. I felt my only option was to find a new career that would afford me the opportunity to prove I was worth my salt. I knew that I had what it took to run a successful business. The challenge was to find someone who would hire me with my recent failure. I had a step hill to climb.

I accredit the stress of wondering how I was going to support my family with the instigation to my baldness. No longer was there talk about maintaining a lavish lifestyle; we were talking about simply living, stress-free.

I tried to ease the blow of business loss and bankruptcy with the rationalization that over five thousand similar family owned businesses in North America had failed in the previous two years. I had reduced debt and tightened the belt, but falling sales and profit margins won over. Hindsight wasn't helpful, knowing we had the chance to sell the business at its peak, but chose not to. And so, painful learning in tow, I attempted to pick up and move on.

When I was young, standing on my tip toes and peering over the fence imagining the glorious life of success that was mine to capture, I most definitely hadn't pictured a road filled with so many obstacles. And yet, for as many hurdles as I had already experienced, the active life of chasing opportunities with mounds of energy, drive and determination had also brought forth plenty of valuable lessons and the revelation of more personal truths.

When there was no money available to continue playing entrepreneur, I had no choice but to find a big job working for someone else. It landed me square in the front page news yet again, as the one who took a stance against the board of directors in the name of not wanting play political games. In truth, I learned that I most definitely did not enjoy waiting (on politics); it was the grandest form of torture for someone living with ADD. I wanted control in my destiny. I wanted it *all, now*!

I grew very aware of just how intently I loved, not just work, but the people in my life. Family was one arena that forever had my attention, and full appreciation. My wife had lost her job the same week I lost mine. She kept me around. We stood there, together, income-less with two boys to raise.

There was a relentless pursuit of success woven to the core of who I was. My wife and I pulled the pieces back together and decided to start another business, in the area of sales distribution. Sadly, I learned the same lesson as the first business, when a technology shift ascended upon us much sooner than expected. The business freight train had my number, and it found me again. The business collapse humbled my pride. We sold the business (at a loss) before things got worse.

Before my eyes, the investment of my time, family resources and a lot of heart was vanishing. Two businesses in five years, gone. One high-profile job firing achieved, and some front page publicity to boot. I never thought that the trend denoted something internal to me, but as life has it, my lessons continued to come forth, until I fully learned them.

And so, I began again, and my next job initiated some real awareness in my life. Having been hired by a large American corporation, I was asked to attend a conference of theirs. There, I met the man who truly opened my eyes to life with ADD. Tom was giving a lecture and held my full, undivided attention for two days. This was unheard of – a full 180 from the young boy in me who couldn't sit through a television program or full class growing up. I approached Tom to let him know that he had, to my great surprise, intrigued me and captured my attention.

"I'm ADD," he said. "Aren't we lucky?"

From that encounter came the most amazing conversation of mutual understanding an appreciation for being gifted with the blessing of great intelligence and energy. I was floored. It took me several years to fully grasp and embrace the concept that Tim had presented: ADD was a gift?

In the time that I further processed just what it might mean to be blessed with ADD, I learned a few more lessons and added a few more notches in my belt. The roller coaster of business ventures gained and lost culminated in too much strain on my marriage. My wife and I agreed to divorce, out of love. It seemed like the only fair thing to do. There I was, forty-nine years of age, divorced and broke.

Another job opportunity came along, and it quickly went after just a year and a half. I questioned if I would ever be able to turn my life around. I then did what I knew best, and started another company. I did so knowing that if I failed, it was now only me that I would be hurt. Sadly, the business concept seemed to be several years ahead of its time, and I had amassed three failed businesses to my name in twenty-five years. Somehow, I still had the drive to believe that *someday* I would get it right. That was, right after I attempted to make work out of my life-long passion and became part a yachting business with two partners. That one didn't come through as I had envisioned either, as feeling undervalued led me to quit. I sold my shares for a profit and attempted to keep moving forward.

I was fifty-four years old and out of work. I was faithful, loving and impulsive…and still looking for the means by which to balance the components of who I was, in order to see success in business. It was introspective work that may very well have saved me. Gaining true, unwavering awareness of my energy, drive and intellect as a gift to the world, made me slow down…in a way. My whole life, the abundant energy of my ADD seemed to drive me. It drove me to chase success. If it was big and shiny, I wanted it. Something amazing happened when I finally decided to stop chasing and simply surrendered to knowing that I had amazing gifts to share: success and abundance found me!

I had a perfect job handed to me over dinner with my two best friends – both accomplished businessmen. It was a sales management role with the stability and flexibility I wanted, and knew I needed. I wouldn't be over-managed, and could retain control of my destiny, alongside that of the company. Those I worked with trusted me to have my own self-discipline and a good work ethic. I was given a challenge, and that in itself made me the right guy for the job. My income was directly related to my efforts and the full use of my intellectual capabilities. What a gift. With time and this new opportunity in front of me, I found the key to my success was in helping entrepreneurs grow their business through the value of outsourcing, and a willingness to delegate and ask for help.

I have learned the language and facets of business through both my professional and personal experience. One of the biggest of those lessons is to delegate the tasks which simply do not fit who I am, or align with the blessings of my ADD. In the same respect, I am also willing to ask for help, and know that while I can control my own destiny, I don't have to create it alone. I can work for someone else and still feel the entrepreneurial spirit within me being forever fueled by energetic drive and determination that are compliments of being gifted with ADD.

Something amazing happens when we surrender to life and all of its lessons. For years, I fought to stay afloat, whether in my own business, working for a large corporation, or seeing the world thru the eyes of a luxurious yachting facility. Now, I find myself enjoying the ride on a more modest ship that can gracefully cast me through the big waves of life, guiding me to a few treasures out in the seas of opportunity.

Once I surrendered to no longer chasing success, the trend of success finding me grew, like the waves casting in treasures of the sea. A business owner who was a customer of mine found his world crumbling down and was in dire straits. I did what any intently loving, good natured, fellow entrepreneur would do: I offered to be of any assistance I could. I had been where he was, struggling, and I lived to tell about it. Through my coaching and guidance, my client now has a successful business. I was able to save him the grief and struggle that I endured, and could help him deal with the inevitable, sooner rather than later.

Perhaps my struggles in business were an inevitable part of my journey. I began to see all too clearly how they had all led to the knowledge and compassionate understanding that I could offer others. What a gift: I have a fulfilling day job *and* the chance to live out my life purpose as a coach.

From one new business opportunity stemmed another. Things are very different this time. Success is coming my way without the pressure to take money from it. Gone are the days when I needed to have all things big, shiny and new, driving myself to ceaselessly work to afford such lavish pleasures. My delights are much different now. It is no longer about belonging to the right clubs, but rather about helping the right people turn their lives around. I feel blessed to be welcomed into others' business and personal journeys, and to have the ADD-fueled energy, drive and determination to assist them.

What was once my troubled story as a student who couldn't focus, became my greatest asset as an entrepreneur who could help others cast their sails in a successful direction. For so many years, I chased the dream of being *somebody* ... and I thought that entailed having grown the biggest business and driving the fanciest car. All along, the *somebody* I was meant to be was simply developing inside of me, through all the ups and downs of my life experiences in family and business. He was much different and much more genuine that anything flashy and external.

I have traveled throughout the world and throughout business. I have two sons with amazing careers, wonderful women in their lives, and three grandchildren. All of these gifts came without the need for success or money to afford them. The love of family and ability to support and help others are the true riches.

It was only at the hand of failure that I came to find my riches and victory. I've learned that very little wisdom is gained through success alone. In success, we often say to ourselves, *I would do it a little differently next time.* In going from failure to failure, I have become the *somebody* who I always longed to be ... and so much more. The fuel that kept my drive to success alive over all of these years was believing in myself in spite of the challenges of ADD, and then stepping into the realization that those challenges themselves were in fact gifts.

Success is rarely easy. You have to push past your comfort zone to obtain it. And yet, there is a fine line between pushing and chasing. It was one thing to forever have the relentless drive that ADD afforded me; it was another to let the blessing of ADD be my sidekick, as we steer my humble ship together. For all the ups and downs, successes and failures, gains and losses, I find myself at total peace.

About Paul

BIO:

Paul was born into a family that fostered success and being the best you could be, no matter the situation. His ADD caused many hard years in school, and difficult decision processes in business. He endured business failures and job losses over thirty years that would have knocked many people of their path, but not Paul.

His desire to be a success was realized after a chance meeting with a business trainer and fellow ADD when he told Paul, "Aren't we lucky to be ADD?" That perspective helped Paul to harness his relentless energy and intelligence as gifts. He is now the Vice President of Answer 365 – a Canadian call center, and is a business coach to budding entrepreneurs. He is currently writing a book of his business life that will be released in the fall of 2016 and will encompass his experiences and what he learned in business. His foundation, no matter the situation, is about building trust that supports his credibility.

Website: www.toyourfuturesuccess.ca

Paul R. Roy

Kelly Falardeau

HIT:

A burn survivor at age two, Kelly's wet diaper may have saved her life, but it did not protect her from growing up as that ugly scar-faced girl struggling to cling to self-esteem and confidence in the face of staring, teasing and rejection.

GIFT:

Kelly is on a global mission as a single mother, speaker and bestselling author to help people live shame-free regardless of outward appearances and unconditionally love themselves by embracing their true beauty and strength.

Passion, Purpose and Beauty

− *KELLY FALARDEAU*

In 1968, I was a cheerful, outgoing toddler, running around in diapers. On August 28th of my second year, I received my hit. Because I was too young to recount it, the story is best told in a letter that my mother wrote me years later.

> *Dear Kel,*
>
> *This is the hardest letter that I have ever had to write. You should realize that August 28, 1968 was the biggest life-changing day of my life. There was nothing that I could do to change that horrible day, no matter what. It was only fifteen minutes in time that, no matter what, could never be changed. How horrible, I couldn't apologize, plead, beg, and bribe my way out of this terrifying accident. It was the most painful, hurtful, go-to-hell-and-back day.*
>
> *I had just had your cousins Michael and Rod in for supper, and you all wanted to go back outside. The boys wanted to keep throwing the old shingles off of the garage roof into the burning barrel. If only I had kept you back to change your diaper. If only, if only, if only, I could say it a million times, but it would still not change anything that happened to you.*
>
> *I heard the boys making noise and you crying. Our neighbour Willie had just driven into the yard. I ran outside to see*

what was going on and you were on the steps at Nana's house. Your shirt was still on fire, so I put my hand on it and put it out. Willie had poured the water on you that Rod had gotten to put out the fire. The boys said you were on the far side of the burning barrel and came around the barrel and were on fire. They didn't want to roll you in the dirt that would make you dirty, so Rod went to get water.

You were crying and crying. It was horrible. I picked you up and ran with you to our house, wrapped a blanket around you, and away you, Uncle Willie and I went to the hospital.

We arrived at emergency and called Dr Ringham to come to the hospital. Dr Ringham saw you and did as much as he could to make you comfortable. He told us to take you as fast as we could to the University of Alberta Hospital. He would call ahead and let them know we were coming. They also called the police for an escort, but we never found them.

We drove so fast that it only took us twenty minutes from Stony Plain Hospital to the University of Alberta Hospital. Normally, it takes forty-five. On the way, you said to me, "Mommy it hurts." That just ripped my heart out and threw it on the floor.

Crying all the while, I replied, "Yes I know baby. We are getting you help as soon as possible." The three of us were terrified.

Three doctors and multiple nurses were all waiting for us when we arrived at the hospital. The doctor scooped you out of my arms and I never saw you again until the next day. Someone took me and put me into an office in the emergency area and forgot about me. All I could do was pray, pray and pray, I was so frightened. I knew nothing for hours.

Finally, after about three hours, Dr. Henry Shimizu came into the room where I was and told me what was going on, where you were, and how seriously you were burned. I don't really have a clue as to what he said other than telling me you had a 50/50 chance of living. All I could imagine was someone flipping a coin saying heads you live, tails you lose.

They took you up to surgery to put a tracheotomy in your throat so you could breathe. Seventy-five percent of your body was burned and thirty-five percent was into the flesh, beyond third degree. The doctor then left me. I didn't see him again for days. I was flabbergasted. I was in shock. I just could not understand why this would happen. What had I done to deserve such punishment? Was it because I was such a rebellious teenager? But, if that was the case, why punish my two-year-old child? Why not me? I wanted to change places with you, and would have, if I could have. It was just insane. All alone, with no one anywhere… what was I to do? My brain was going a one-hundred miles per hour. Where were my parents, my husband – someone to rescue me, wake me up and tell me it was all a bad dream? It couldn't be true. Terrible things don't happen to people like us. I could not make heads nor tails of what, in heaven's name, was going on. It was so unbelievable.

Please God, I asked, what can I do to change this horrible tragedy? What, when, why and how do I change this? I don't know what to do. What about my beautiful baby Kelly Ann? My beautiful baby. Please God, don't take her from me. I just got her two years ago. Don't take this baby away from me too. Kelly is so wonderful, happy, smiley, so pure, so good, so innocent. Why my child? She is the only good thing in my life and you want to take her away from me, I don't understand. Why is life so cruel? What's going on? This is terrifying. Please stop the world and let me off. Let me go back to yesterday, I will do anything to change this day. What can I do? Panic was not the word for what I was feeling.

Finally, your dad found me. It was around midnight or so. He wanted to know what happened. He wanted to kill the boys. Well, it took a lot of talking to stop that from happening.

The nurses would not let us see you because you were in the operating room and they didn't know when you would be in a bed. They took our phone number and said they would call if anything happened. We left the hospital in shock. Your dad drove home. We were both bargaining with God to change things, but no dice. This couldn't be happening. On the way home the song "You are my Precious Angel" came on the radio. I was crying my eyes out. To this day, I still cry when I hear that song. I can now play it on the piano, but it takes a lot to stop the tears.

Lots of love, Mom

I was only two years old when I was burned. The extent of my injuries and the number of procedures I have endured over the years are lengthy. Seventy-five percent of my body was burned that August day in 1968, and fifty-five percent of the burns were third degree. I spent four months in the hospital. Twice a week, the doctors would take me to the operating room to do what surgeries needed to be done. They didn't want to put me in any more pain than I already was, so they would put me to sleep to take my stitches out.

Every second year thereafter, until I was twenty years old, I would spend a month in the hospital. When I was three, my arm contracted and joined right to my body, so my doctor had to cut it away from my body and put me in a body cast, so that my arm couldn't fall back into my body and contract again. I've had many skin grafts, using the skin on my legs six times over. I also had breast surgery when I was sixteen, because my one breast was quite a bit lower than the other. One breast was also missing a nipple, because it had been burned off. My doctor took the skin from both sides of my one leg and put it under both of my breasts, affixing them in the right place so they would be even. At that time of the surgery, my doctor used staples to hold the skin together. There were approximately one thousand staples in my breasts. I still remember having to go back to the hospital to get the staples taken out.

From a very young age, I had to deal with people staring at me all the time. I remember going to the mall and getting annoyed that people were staring at me. I would turn around so they couldn't take a second or third look. Every time, I would deal with it differently. Sometimes I would stick my tongue out at the kid or give them a dirty look. Sometimes I would say, "What are you staring at?" Every time varied, depending on my mood.

When I was a kid, I just wanted to be accepted and beautiful. I just wanted to blend in with everyone else. I didn't want people to notice my scars and think I was ugly. I wanted to be considered normal, not different. I wanted to forget I was burnt. Because I didn't remember my accident, I tried everything I could to convince myself that it didn't happen…but looking down at my arms quickly brought me back to the reality that I really had been in an accident that made me ugly. I just wanted to be able to walk through a bunch of kids and be considered normal and pretty for once.

Growing up as a teenager, being burnt and labelled as the ugly scar-faced girl seemed to mean that I would never be beautiful. I used to hate models because they were beautiful, and I wasn't. As far as I was concerned, anybody else could be beautiful. All they had to do was put on some makeup, do up their hair and put on a great outfit with some heels and they'd be beautiful. I believed that I could never be beautiful, because I had ugly scars that would never go away.

I'll never forget the last time my mom and I went to my plastic surgeon. Every two years, I would go to his office and have to take all my clothes off so he could look at my body and decide what had to be done next. The great thing about my physical growth was that it meant I had more skin to work with. That is precisely why I had to wait every two years before having more reconstructive surgery. Every time, I hoped there would be some magic procedure to take my scars away and make me beautiful…and then, my dream was crushed. The doctor told me he had done everything he could and there was nothing more he could do. There were no further surgeries that could take my ugly scars away. The only option left for me was to wear make-up to cover up my scars. I hated make-up. I hated the feel of it, and I hated the fact that I would have to spend an hour every day applying it just to look beautiful. I didn't want to wear a mask. People would still know I was burnt, because I still had scars everywhere else. So why cover the ones on my face?

When I was eighteen, I decided that I had to know why I had lived through the tragedy. I got hypnotized in hopes that I could figure it out. I went back to two days in my life: the day I got burnt and the day I died in the hospital. The day I died in the hospital, I had an outer-body experience and was above my bed watching the doctors and nurses scramble as they were doing everything they could to save my life. As they tried to save me, there I was, above my body, having a conversation with my God about why I should live. He said I should live because I was too young to die. We talked some more. I then asked again, "But why?" He told me it was because I needed to live for my grandpa and sister. I then said, "Okay, I'll live," and I came back to life.

As I grew older, I longed to know my purpose in life. My grandpa told me that he knew I wouldn't die. His pastor of the church told him that there had to be a reason I lived, and that I had a purpose. Why did a two-year-old who was burnt in 1968 to seventy-five percent of her body survive? That was my question to answer.

I've had a couple of critical turning points in my life. The first was in eighth grade. I remember looking at all the girls in their jeans. At that point, I was still wearing handmade clothes that my grandma made me. I remembered talking to my best friend at the time and telling her that I didn't like the jeans I was wearing. She said, "Well, get new ones." That's when I thought, hey, just because I'm the ugly scar-faced girl doesn't mean that I don't deserve to wear what the popular girls are wearing. From that day, I started babysitting and saving up my money so that I could buy my own clothes.

Another turning point came years later, when my ex-husband and I went to a garage sale. I was looking around when an older lady said to me, "They couldn't do better than that?" I remember thinking, *oh my goodness,*

I haven't been called ugly in years. How could she say something so rude? I had a little talk with myself and thought about what I was going to say in return. Should I be a bitch and be rude back to her? No, I didn't handle things that way anymore (even though I used to when I was a kid). She surely didn't deserve the 'nice Kelly' response though. I turned back to her and said, "I happen to think I look pretty damn good," and I walked out.

I was hurt, extremely hurt. The older woman didn't know how I got burnt, or what I looked like before all my surgeries. She didn't know I had had surgeries every two years until I was twenty years old. She didn't know how my scars had faded over the years. She knew nothing, and yet, she found something so rude to say to me.

I started questioning why I was allowing a complete stranger to take my power away. Why was I letting this woman make me feel ugly when I would likely never see her ever again? Not once had my family or friends said, "Kel, we would love you more if you didn't have scars on your face." That was when I realized that this woman's opinion didn't count in my world, and I truly allowed myself to feel beautiful about myself. I stepped into the realization that nobody's opinion but my own counted. That was a pivotal day in my emotional transformation from feeling like 'the ugliest person in the world,' to claiming my personal power and beauty.

A third turning point in my life was the acceptance that I needed to be a speaker. I had met Charmaine Hammond, a respected professional speaker and facilitator, at a business mixer. She told me that I needed to be a speaker, and that people would be really inspired by my story. I replied stating that I didn't have a story, and that I was just a burn survivor. Persistent, Charmaine asked an interviewer friend of hers if she could squeeze in a time slot for me to speak with her on her show and share my story. As I was speaking during the interview, I noticed some people laughing. I remembered wondering why were they laughing. I looked on the stage and realized that I was the only one speaking. As I continued sharing, I noticed people crying. I questioned why they were crying. I looked on the stage once again and noticed I was the only one speaking. That was when I realized that they were all laughing and crying at my stories. I really could impact people.

Charmaine decided she had to step it up a notch and helped me just a little bit more by inviting me to volunteer at the event she was hosting, where charismatic Janet Attwood would be showcasing her *Passion Test*. I wanted to discover what my passions were. I didn't yet understand why my story was special.

During the seminar, I completed the passion test. Janet took me by my arms and said "Kelly, your scars are your gift, use them. Be a speaker and inspire others." I agreed that I would accept that I should be a speaker and just do it. It took me a lot of strength to step into recognition that I could be an inspiration to others.

Ever since I accepted that I could be a speaker and positively impact others, things have fallen into place almost magically. Today, I'm an international speaker and bestselling author of four books: *No Risk No Rewards, Self Esteem Doesn't Come in a Bottle, 1000 Tips for Teenagers* and *7 Reasons Women Don't Love Themselves and How to Change It*. I have been to Africa twice to work with the burn survivors there. I won the Fierce Woman Award, along with the YWCA Woman of Distinction and the Queen Elizabeth II Diamond Jubilee medal. I'm currently working on my next book, *Still Beautiful*, and creating an accompanying companion documentary.

About Kelly

BIO:

Kelly Falardeau is a burn survivor. Since the age of two, she has struggled with her self-worth and confidence after receiving burns to seventy-five percent of her body. Kelly found a way to go from near-death to success, and from seeing herself as *the ugly scar-faced girl* to being one of the Top 10 Most Powerful and Influential Speakers, a Fierce Woman of the Year, a best-selling author, and a recipient of the both Queen Elizabeth II Diamond Jubilee Medal and YWCA Woman of Distinction 2013 awards. Her written works include *No Risk, No Rewards, Self-Esteem Doesn't Come in a Bottle*, and *1000 Tips for Teenagers*.

Website: www.kellyfalardeau.com

Kelly Falardeau

Thomas Cantley

HIT:

The world yelled "Cut!" in the story of Thomas's life, as he was halted in his career as a high flying filmmaker & photographer in New York by the diagnosis of stage III testicular cancer.

GIFT:

Through a shift in paradigm, Thomas used his Ballsy approach to life to propel the documentary footage of his ordeal with testicular cancer in to a worldwide revolution for the education and awareness of men's health.

I Am Ballsy
– *THOMAS CANTLEY*

And, roll it.

It was in my early twenties that I discovered a real passion for being behind the camera; and within a few short years, I landed an elite job with one of the world's most prestigious photography agencies. I fully expected an immediate offer to shoot on the red carpet at the Emmys, so you can imagine the bitter taste of disdain when I was assigned a job of shooting a lowly CD release party at a classy dive bar (*yes*, they exist) in New York's lower east side.

I dragged myself to that shoot, ego wailing, with intentions of getting a drink, getting the shot and then getting the hell out of there. And when the star of the party, Katy, excitedly greeted me, I hardly gave her the time of day. Long before getting to the shoot, I had decided that I didn't *want* to be there.

Well, as it turns out, that little CD release party was for an artist by the name of Katy Perry, and her new release "I Kissed a Girl" went all the way to number one on the Billboard charts.

Fast forward to just over a year later. The scene was much different: a sterile isolated room, enclosed by four bare walls and some sadly outdated decor, or total lack thereof. There were no bright lights, no potent cocktails, and no wild after-parties.

I sat on the on the edge of a brown leather couch that was wrapped in plastic of a strangely adhesive nature, with fear of the unknown impurities left on its surface by those who had frequented the room before me.

There was an eerie silence of anxiety and anticipation that I did my best to completely ignore.

I had been cast the lead role in the shocking documentary that had become my life. And in this shot, I had been instructed to provide a sperm sample that would determine my fate and the ongoing nature of my being diagnosed with testicular cancer, in a room that showed little respect for my current situation.

People knew me as a brutally honest photographer and filmmaker, with a critical eye for what needed to be changed. New York's finest came out for Katy Perry's CD release party before anyone even knew who she was; and yet I, a twenty-six year old testicular cancer patient, was hastily handed some tasteless 1970s style pornography and given a creepy, depressing lair in which to masturbate. The treatment of men's health was in need of a massive overhaul.

Flashback: A scene inserted into the present time that deals with the past.

The pre-cancer me was a ruthless filmmaker and photographer living the high life in New York, both literally and metaphorically. I was willing to do anything to get on top. Working with celebrities on a regular basis did wonders for my ego and provided ample social opportunities for the party boy – and correspondingly, often the life of the party – that I was. I thought that I had it all; and yet, I really didn't give a damn about the value of my own life. I guess riding the high was much like being high, everything looked rosy and super cool, until the high wore off and it all came crashing down.

When you're living a life based on the demands of celebrities, and Katy Perry wants you to shoot her CD release party, you don't really (think you) have time to take care of your health, let alone get sick. And when you're life has gone from the highest of highs to the lowest of lows, and you're living on the streets of New York street-performing for money until a friend takes you in to sleep on her floor (*yes*, that happened... but that's an entire other book in itself), there definitely isn't room (or money) to take care of your testicle when it begins to swell to the point of being an obvious abnormality.

If I wasn't in excruciating pain, I wasn't going to stop and worry about what was going on with my body. And if there was pain, there was usually a drug for that.

You know those situations where you wonder how the heck your life got to that point? Well, that wasn't one of them. Had I looked at anyone else in my situation, I would have thought *that's a nightmare*, but it's amazing what stubborn determination will do to push you forward...at least until such point where you can actually no longer move.

Ignorance was bliss, until the day that I actually could not fit my pants over my balls. Well, one ball, and one testicle swollen to the size of an orange. I could hardly walk. If you've ever had a fruit basket dumped in your pants, then you know what I'm talking about. I called my astronomically enlarged testicle *the mutant*, and I wanted it removed *stat*.

The only way to get me to go *to* the hospital was to have been driven to a point where I absolutely, without question, *had* to be hospitalized. The doctors gladly pumped me full of morphine and hydromorphone – an even more potent painkiller cocktail than its brother morphine. I became a bit like a fast paced race car – they would fuel me up with hydromorphone, send me home, and tell me to come back to the *emergency pit stop* when I needed to refuel (i.e. when the high from the painkillers began to wear off). Given that I really didn't feel that I had time for all that shit, I would stagger back to the hospital only after the high had worn off...or I ended up with testicle torsion (a painful twist of the spermatic cord which cuts off all blood circulation to the testicle). That was precisely the case on my third visit back to the emergency room.

Being an immigrant to the United States, I was sent to the Bellevue Hospital in New York, with all of the other immigrants...and a few prison inmates thrown into the mix. The hallways of the hospital would have scared the shit out of most people, but I (high as a kite on hydromorphone) chose to see it as just more great documentary footage. I may have spent some time living on the streets, but I never stopped being a filmmaker.

If only I had my camera ready the night that I awoke to the site of a dark skinned E.T. like creature, hand cuffed to her IV, asking me for matches or change. For a second I had to remember that I was not on the streets of Harlem, but in fact in the *questionable* safety of a hospital bed. I was later told that the girl who had hovered over my bed in the middle of the night was a pyromaniac and had already set herself on fire several times, to the effect of suffering severe burns that had forever distorted her face. I felt no reassurance knowing that she and her IV walked the hospital halls in search of matches to introduce to a local oxygen tank, or other flammable substance.

There was also an Irish woman staying in the room next to me. Her terminal cancer left her screaming in pain for hours on end—cries that went unanswered by any of the nursing staff. Being immigrants, none of us was equipped with proper health care coverage to pay for the hospital's services, and the staff obviously knew it. In that moment, something came over me. There was nothing in me that would have this Irish woman be simply left to die in pain. I marched out to the nurses' station and *demanded* that someone take care of the screaming woman. I recall a rather unfamiliar feeling coming over me in that moment. It was a sense of caring for someone else....

Cut: Marks a rapid transition from one time space to another.

The doctors gladly obliged and removed my left testicle (aka *the mutant*) during my stay in hospital. And just before surgery they so kindly advised me that they had previously misdiagnosed, and the cause of my orange-sized testicle was actually stage III (nearly stage IV) testicular cancer. Did I care? Nope. I wanted *the mutant* gone...and a few more hours of film footage would be great too. All that really mattered is that I no longer had to hobble around with that damn orange in my pants. That was, until just over a week later, when the pain ensued and I found myself with a round-trip ticket back to the halls of Bellevue. The verdict: my cancer had spread to my lymph nodes and I needed immediate surgery. I vaguely remember the doctors mumbling something about it being necessary if I wanted to live....

Pan North.

Heading back up north to Halifax, Nova Scotia, Canada was the only feasible option for me to take care of having a retroperitoneal lymphadenectomy (also known as RPLND surgery, and just about as glorious as it sounds). After finally disclosing to my mother the ruckus that had become my life, she flew to New York and escorted me back to Halifax. I no longer had to go it all alone. I now had a production assistant.

You may laugh, but that was pretty much the truth of it. I filmed *everything;* like your friendly neighbourhood creeper armed with a video camera. I treated myself like a third party, capturing great and not so great shots of everything from my trips to the hospital and my tripping on hydromorphone, to a narrative play-by-play of my days with testicular cancer. No need to take the time to absorb the fact that I had just received a stage III diagnosis, I had a documentary to make. And when the doctor's assistant called to book my second surgery, I told her that I would like to get it all on film. She so eloquently told me that would not be possible because of the risk of introducing infection by bringing my camera in to the hospital. I bluntly replied that I would then not be coming in for my surgery, until such time when they decided that I could film it all.

While I may have been ruthless and self-centered in my pre-cancer days, the assertiveness and drive that I had did carry some clout going forth. A few hours later I received a call from the doctor's assistant, stating that I would be able to film my time in the hospital for my second surgery.

I captured full footage of the procedure preparation...with help from my production assistant, of course. And when it came time for the surgery, I set the camera up myself in the operating room, ensured that I was properly framed in the shot, laid down on the operating table and allowed the doctors to cut me open. My filming stopped at nothing. It came first. And when the staples from the incisions all the way up my abdomen ripped open to holes the size of large coins, I would not allow the doctor to patch them back up until I was able to capture footage on camera, no matter how much blood was pissing out of me.

As it turned out, the doctor won that fight. I couldn't get the camera in time and he refused to allow me to bleed to death. I suppose it is good to run into people who are more assertive than you when your mission becomes *mildly* self-destructive.

My trip to Halifax concluded with more great film footage. There were shots of me in every hospital situation imaginable, and some perhaps not so imaginable (please see earlier *70s porn room* story). There were meetings with doctors and surgeons, and there was even an interview with a nineteen year old testicular cancer patient in hospital with me. In total, more than a documentary's worth of video footage was in my possession. And as soon as I could physically get out of bed on my own, you better believe I was on the first flight back to New York. I, the acclaimed filmmaker and photographer, had a career to reset, and one hell of a lot of (hydromorphone infused) footage to go through.

Editing: Pulling shots together to make up the film.

Like any good film editor, I should probably have taken the time to fully digest the content of the footage I had. But short of a few breakdowns, I really didn't take the time to fully accept that I had testicular cancer, or to understand what having it meant to me. After all, the filmmaker in me had work to do.

Using some of the discernable footage that I had (i.e. that which did not involve me hyped up on hydromorphone), I began to do what came naturally -- I began to blog and post videos. After all, I had one heck of a story. I figured *someone* would watch it.

As I pushed forward, the impact of my two-month long whirlwind experience began to sink in. There were days when I truly felt down. There were days when my big idea to create a documentary of my ordeal seemed hindered by financial burdens. And then there was the day that I found within the strength to create a minute long video – a trailer for the film that would detail my struggle with testicular cancer. That was the day that everything changed.

Within a few weeks of posting the video on You Tube, I received a message from a nineteen year old man in New Zealand. He posted a note stating that my video gave him the courage to go and get himself checked; and if it hadn't been for my video, he may not have discovered that he *had* testicular cancer. Early detection saved his life, and in a way, he had saved mine. Everything shifted in that moment. My life became more real. One young voice from the other side of the world had given me the courage to forge ahead.

I'm happy for you was all I could muster through tears on a follow up video post directed at the young man whose story changed my life forever. And to all the other viewers I proclaimed: *go check yourself.* That day I morphed (at a much more conscious pace than my days spend *hydromorphing*) from a filmmaker who was just going to make a documentary about his ordeal, to a man who was going to ensure that the world would be different because I was in it. Still true to the person I had always been, I stayed edgy and innovative; and my videos and blog posts began to resound with others. From all over the world, people began to send personal messages about being able to relate to my nightmare.

Inspired by the outcry for lacking support, I created the Ballsy Cancer Society, and over the course of a few years helped raise thousands of dollars for cancer research. While partnering with other cancer related organizations was empowering, I wanted more. I wanted to create a movement, an awareness, a *revolution*.

I saw a gap between raising funds for cancer research and a true understanding of where those funds were going. It was the message of *awareness* in my video that had saved a young man's life in New Zealand. That was where I needed to focus.

Reverse Angle: A shot from the opposite side of a subject.

I don't know that I've yet fully digested the impact that having cancer had on my life, and it has now been three years since I was declared in remission. I can, however, state with great certainty that cancer was the best thing that ever happened to me. While I'm still discovering the extent to which that statement holds true, I am glad that I got cancer because of the person it has helped me become. Once brash and self-centered, I wanted to be a huge movie director...before cancer stopped me in my tracks. The sweet irony: the filmmaker in me has captured footage that will create arguably one of the most real and raw documentaries that I could ever have imagined making. And all that compliments of reality, and a big orange in my pants.

If you were to ask me if I have totally changed since the hit of stage III testicular cancer in my life, I would absolutely say *yes*. And if you were to ask me if there were anything that I would change about the ordeal itself, I would resoundingly say *no*. My focus has done a *180*, from me-focused to purpose-driven. A life that was once about me on the red carpet capturing celebrities in their best light is now about helping shed light on the indisputable need for awareness and openness of men's health.

What has remained the same, however, is my drive and willingness to take big risks. I am not afraid to be vocal and use a healthy dose of reality to spread the message of helping men become aware of their health and screen themselves for illnesses like testicular cancer. Touching the world via speaking engagements, online videos, a documentary and a book (or several!), I am grasping my full potential and using it to spread a life-changing message. I'll do whatever it takes to help any boy or man to keep himself from ending up with a cancer as far advanced as mine was. I won't appear by your bedside asking for matches or change in the middle of the night, but I will be raw and honest in ask for your listening ear.

Being healthy and happy now come first. I'll never let any problems in my life grow to the size of an orange and leave me unable to move forward before I take note and deal with them. I am aware of my body, and on a mad mission to help other men become more aware of theirs.

I may now be one testicle short, but I will be forever Ballsy.

About Thomas

BIO:

Thomas Cantley has lived his entire life with an eye for opportunity. He was granted an education as a filmmaker at the elite Vancouver Film School, and celebrities came to know him by name as a New York City photographer. That was precisely when an opportunity of unexpected proportions found him – as chronicling his struggles with stage III testicular cancer led to his real purpose.

Today, Thomas dedicates all of his time to ensuring that no man will have to endure the health horror he did. He has created his own cancer society and raised funds with the biggest cancer organizations in the world. He has started a *Ballsy* movement, singlehandedly pushing a giant ball (testicle) over 7000 miles across two countries. His vision of raising awareness for men's health has landed him nearly 300 media appearances, including being featured in *The Doctors, Huffington Post, Today, Men's Health, Cosmo, Esquire, Fox* and *ABC*.

Website: www.thomascantley.com

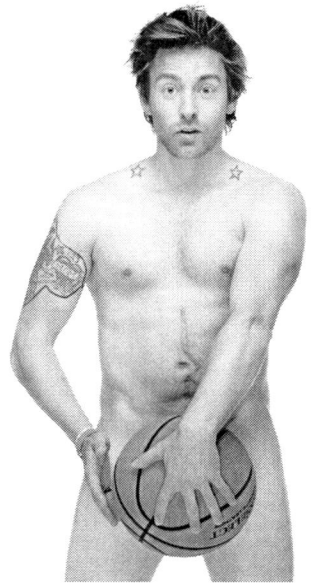

Thomas Cantley

Kathy Jourdain

HIT:

Helplessly watching her vibrant mother's descent into a diminishing world of dementia, Kathy made the heart-wrenching decision to commit her mother to the corridors of death and dying of a nursing home at the young age of seventy-six.

GIFT:

Kathy looked into her mother's eyes the night she died with a peaceful, grateful heart knowing her human tragedy story was transformed through the perspective of soul journey. Kathy has now forever shifted the shape of her life as a consultant and author to help others make new meaning of their life experiences.

Soul Journey
Beyond Human Tragedy
– *KATHY JOURDAIN*

My mother continued to tell me that her breast prosthesis had broken down. While she had complained to me about it, I hadn't seen it, nor did I ask to see it. I did not hear her through the dementia lens I had put on her. I thought she was rambling and I discredited her…until a few weeks later. It was then that my father, mother and I found ourselves sitting in one of their many medical appointments. This one was for my father. As we waited, my mother reached into her bra and pulled out the prosthesis. It had broken down and was sticky. My eyes widened in alarm, shock and dismay. In that moment, I felt disappointed in myself for not seeing past the human tragedy story of dementia, for dismissing my mother, and for casting aside her intelligence and awareness. Thankfully, she was persistent.

Rather than buy a new prosthesis, we decided to go bra shopping, thinking that my mother could stuff the left side of her bra with tissue. She had a habit, born through the increasing haze of dementia, of collecting tissue and tucking it away all over the place anyway. There were bundles of folded tissue under her pillow, in drawers, in her purse and under things.

While in the dressing room at a women's dress shop in Lunenburg, N.S., my mother took off her blouse to try on a bra. She looked down at her chest, puzzled. She looked at the right and the left sides, scanning them both again before finally landing her gaze on her left side.

She then looked at me and said, "This side is kind of flat."

In spite of myself, I laughed. There aren't many choices: laugh or cry. I reminded my mother that she had had her breast removed due to breast cancer. As I watched her expression, I saw both her curiosity and her hesitancy. I wasn't sure she understood. While I shook my head with a mix of consternation and amusement, I was aware that dementia was not just causing my mother to forget recent events and have trouble expressing her thoughts, it was also causing her to forget events from all stages in her life, including when she was young. Her memories were disappearing. She was becoming lost – lost to her own experiences and the stories she used to make meaning of her life, lost to my father who still lived with her and her situation every day, and lost to my brother and me.

Over and over again, I could feel life calling me to consciousness and intentionality. I responded with the imperfectness of my humanity: sometimes well, sometimes less well, sometimes with more awareness, sometimes with less, but always with a growing willingness to be on the edges of my own learning. My mother and her journey with dementia was becoming one of my greatest teachers.

As an occasional visitor to my parents' home, it was harder for me to see the signs of the onset of dementia. As a family, we collaborated, wanting my mother to be well. My brother, Robert, visited for longer periods, and thereby became more aware of the situation and my mother's behavior. My dad, Hector, dealt with my mother's gradual loss of cognitive abilities on an ongoing basis. He would share stories of following her to put the washing machine cover down because she didn't understand why it wouldn't start, or watching her take the banana bread out of the oven after just a few minutes and not understanding why it wasn't cooked.

My parents' fiftieth anniversary coincided with the time we began the process for my mother to enter long-term care. Taking care of her had become an increasing strain on my father. There were all kinds of new idiosyncrasies in her behavior. Once when I visited, she took me upstairs to go through her drawers. She tried to give me back the sweaters I had given her as birthday and Christmas presents. When we came back downstairs, she went into the living room and brought out a beautiful figurine of a woman dressed in a flowing blue dress.

"Here," she says, "This is yours."

"No," I tell her every time. "It's yours. I gave it to you as a gift."

This became a regular pattern whenever I visited.

When we began the process of finding long-term care, we were told it would take six to nine months to have my mother placed in a home. As we began the process, I told dad, "You know, when they call, she will have to go. We won't be able to say no, or she will go back to the bottom of the list and we'll have to start all over again."

It's a whole different story when you get the call. Just five months later, it came, and within a week we were moving my mother out of her home of more than thirty years and into a little shared room at Harbourview Haven, where people move when they are preparing to die. She never wanted to go there. No one ever does. There is only one way out. It was one of the most heartbreaking decisions I have ever had to participate in, and easily the most difficult decision we have ever made as a family. We all tried to hold back the tears. As we prepared to leave her for the first time, my mother followed us out to the door, ready to go home with us. I'll never forget her staring at us, confused as to why she was being left behind.

For the first year, my father visited my mother daily, until he was encouraged to live his life as best he could under the circumstances. He then began to visit a little less frequently, though still loyally. I visited when I could.

Every time I entered the residential part of the home, my senses were assaulted. I came upon people – old people and in some cases, really old people – sitting in wheel chairs or chairs – just sitting for the most part, most of them nodding off. Those were the ones well enough to be sitting up. In most of the rooms, someone was lying on a bed, oblivious to the rest of the world. And, as good as this facility is, it smelled of people waiting to die. I would make my way through multiple locked doors to get to the dementia unit. As I walk through, I often wondered what the meaning of life is when you are so old and incapacitated, just waiting to die, or living in your own little demented world? It was a human tragedy. It made no sense.

I witnessed my mother go from walking, to sitting in a wheelchair, to moving less and less. When she opened her mouth to speak, a few words would come out, but the thought would disappear and she could not complete a sentence. When I acted like what she had said didn't make sense, she became stressed. When I pretended that everything was fine and struck a rapport with my mother, she was in good humor. I reconciled she was no longer the woman who raised me. I needed to be present to the woman who was standing, or sitting, before me.

As my mother began to speak less and less, and her thoughts were jumbled and incoherent, she brightened up when she saw people she knew and loved. When I would walk into the dementia ward, her eyes would light up. Did she know I was her daughter? I don't know. She knew that she knew me, and she knew that she loved me. It is this language of love that caused me to shift perspective on my mom and her dementia. Instead of judging her situation, I began to observe more and become curious.

The human story is tragic. I bemoaned the decisions that need to made on behalf of my mother, in relation to her care. I never wanted my children to have to make those decisions on my behalf. I told my boys that if we all begin to notice signs of dementia or Alzheimer's in me when I'm older, I would try to take matters into my own hands before it is too late. I am not afraid of death. I am afraid of becoming the living dead, haunting the corridors of death and dying, as a shell of who I was.

My mother's journey with dementia invited me fully into the exploration of perspective of our lives – one of human tragedy or soul journey. I had always thought that I viewed her journey, my journey, or anyone's journey, from the perspective of the soul. This was true, to a certain degree. I wondered what it would take to understand my mother's situation differently. The perspective of soul journey began to capture my attention in a new way. Nothing else made sense. Why would an otherwise perfectly healthy individual lose their sense of their life and of who they are? It is senseless from the perspective of physical form. It was precisely that senselessness that took me deeper and deeper into the soul journey perspective.

Because I believe in soul contracts and agreements extending over many life times, I ask different questions. What if, before my mother manifested into human form, she made decisions about what she wanted to experience in this lifetime? What if experiencing decreasing cognitive awareness was a part of her soul exploration? What if this was all a soul choice? How can we know? How could anybody know for sure? Just asking these questions expands possibilities for me, inviting in more compassion and generosity.

As my perspective and curiosity about my mother and her journey expanded, I began to wonder if I could reach her in another way. What if I could shift my consciousness to a different plane – to a meditative state – that touches a more universal consciousness? What might happen then? As I sat with her in her room one visit, I decided to test it. I began to meditate, while keeping my eyes on my mother as she stared out the window. I felt my consciousness shift and my mother turned to look directly at me with an expression of surprise on her face. There was no doubt in my mind, or soul, that I had made contact with her. It was fleeting, but I had awareness of this communication pathway now. I knew that I could do it from anywhere and became increasingly curious about the non-physical component of my mother's journey.

On subsequent visits, I would sit with my mother on her bed, maintaining physical touch the whole time. When she looked at me, we held eye contact. She would smile and even laugh. So did I…sometimes with tears also flowing. The rest of the time, I watched her lift her head to look very intently at things I could not see all around us. It was clear that spirit was gathering, though less clear when she would finally decide to let go of her physical body. That same visit, I had a little revelation – something that had never occurred to me before.

My awareness expanded in relation to what else might be going on in the corridors of death and dying. As I observed my mother looking at that which she could see and I could not, I became aware that her physical body might be old and weak and her brain 'injured,' though her spirit or soul was strong. I was no longer visiting with the personality and ego that inhabited her body for all those years before dementia; I was visiting with her in the spirit of her soul's journey. Looking past her un-brushed teeth, unkempt hair and incoherence, along with my own sorrow for the loss of this vibrant woman and mother in my life, I saw her spirit shine through her eyes with delight when she saw me. Her soul was connecting with my soul. I began to wonder just where, how far, and how often my mother may be journeying while her physical body sleeps or appears unconscious. Such a thought took me to all the sleeping bodies throughout the whole facility. A deeper curiosity had begun to dawn within me. Who is to say that most of the souls staying there were not journeying while they lay asleep? Who is to say that they are not off doing much needed soul work in other dimensions?

The human tragedy story is so apparent it can obliterate the soul journey perspective. It is often hard to see beyond the sights, sounds and smells assaulting your senses, such as those that would stun me as I walked the halls of the home. It was all so blinding, making it almost impossible to see anything beyond the physical. It was nearly impossible to see the fullness and vibrancy that exists just beyond the veil.

Now, I am aware of a bubble of light that surrounds the home. The beautiful souls who live therein might be making contributions to the world that most of us cannot see or understand, and that makes my own spirit more joyful. I now hold my mother's journey with an added degree of lightness and delight, which I have no doubt she feels. I know she is a great teacher for me – a teacher of journey, a teacher of love, and a teacher of dying and death.

When my mother was on the verge of her death, she was transferred to a different room, where I could stay with her. I would sit on the arm of the couch, eye level with her, as she lay in her bed. I looked into her blue eyes, and she held my gaze. For a woman who had been increasingly less present over the last few years, she was just as present as I was in that moment. I was mesmerized, unable to take my gaze away. I talked to her, telling her about things and people in my life. I told her how beautiful she is, and how gifted and loved she is. I thanked her for being in my life, and for being my mom. Most of all, I held her gaze with love.

As I sat with her, I meditated, allowing my consciousness to tune into what more was happening in the moment. I sensed her guides celebrating as they prepared to receive her. There were points of light, shimmering, sparkling and lighting the way. I felt overcome with a feeling of joy. There was such readiness, and it was all calming and beautiful. As my mother lay in the final hours of staying with her physical body, preparing to let go, it was a gift to sit vigil with her.

The staff at The Harbourview Haven home taught me about human dignity and respect in how they related to my mother. Even up to her last moment, they treated her as if she was fully present and aware. They called her by her name. "Mary," they would say, "We're going to turn you over now." "Mary, we are going to give you your meds now." On the morning of her death, a care worker came in to wash my mother's face and freshen her up, providing a depth of love, care, dignity and respect to a woman in her last moments on this physical plane.

On February 8th, 2012, my mother, Mary Patricia Ann Ritcey Jourdain, drew her last breaths before falling quiet at 12:30p.m. Then there was silence, her silence. No longer were there rattling breaths drawn with effort through her lungs into her ravaged body. With her last breaths, I had imagined her spirit gently tugging until the last wisps of it are finally released into a delightful little dance of joy and freedom. Our silence – my brother, father and me – was in reverence for my mother, her journey and the honor of witnessing the final stages of her transition from physical form into spirit.

I have become aware that dying and death requires the same kind of loving care and attention as birth does. It is birth – a birth back to spirit. It happens when the soul is ready...though not necessarily when those who are waiting think it should be. It is much the same as when we await the birth of a newborn, and they arrive on their own timing, not ours.

The night of my mother's passing, I drove back to my own home with the full moon shining brightly. I did not feel sorrow, but rather joy, euphoric joy – just like when my children were born. I drove by the light of the moon and the light of my mother's joyous spirit, free from human form. Her journey illuminated the soul journey perspective for me, amidst a human tragedy story. I am now certain that whatever happens to me, now or later, dementia or other, that it is all part of my soul journey. If I end up in long-term care, or my children have to make choices about my life, it will be okay. I will be okay. They will be okay.

My mother's journey with dementia was a long one. My journey through hers was an inspired one. Learning to see past human tragedy to soul journey, so much more makes sense and so much more richness enters into my life. It is much like my boys shared with me when they were younger and their grandfather on their father's side had just died. They went to the funeral. Afterward I asked them, "How was it for you?"

Children can be so wise. As we began to talk about death, they said to me, "We think it's kind of like this: you know when you dream and when you are in the middle of a dream it seems real, but then you wake up and you know it was just a dream? We think life is like that. It is really just a dream, but it all seems real. Then you die, but dying is really like waking up and realizing it was just a dream."

Personally, I'm dreaming of soul journey these days.

About Kathy

BIO:

Having allowed her consciousness and curiosity for the soul's journey to shape her purpose, Kathy Jourdain is a grounded visionary focused on understanding life. She is co-founder of Worldview Intelligence, where innovative thinking and a deeper understanding of the worldview drive her work. In her role, she focuses on how worldviews are developed and why understanding and working with them creates a fundamentally different environment for today's most challenging conversations. Kathy is also internationally recognized as a steward and practitioner of the Art of Hosting (AoH) Conversations That Matter, which provides a set of patterns and practices to understand and work with complexity in increasingly unpredictable circumstances. Some of her most personal work lies in her memoir: *Embracing the Stranger in Me: A Journey to Openheartedness*. Her deep sharing of her personal journey invites others to enter or stay with their journey.

Websites: www.WorldviewIntelligence.com

www.ShapeShiftstrategies.com

www.KathyJourdain.com

Kathy Jourdain

Louise Levesque-Burley

HIT:

Born with the twin challenges of chronic juvenile arthritis and visual impairment, Louise faced a life of never seeing beyond daily struggle.

GIFT:

Despite her physical limitations, Louise persevered with tenacity, courage and INsight to make her professional speaking and training dreams a reality, as she engages, entertains and educates audiences to make *The Impossible Possible* in their own lives.

The Impossible is Possible
– *LOUISE LEVESQUE-BURLEY*

How do we instill a sense of resilience within ourselves? Does our very existence mean that we defied the odds to be a part of this life? Resilience is said to be the ability to cope with and overcome misfortune or change, and return to one's natural emotional state.

From day one, I was someone who lived to defy the odds. Tell me something is impossible, and I'll show you that it is possible.

My mother was three months pregnant and my parents eagerly awaiting my arrival, when their doctor sternly advised them that the pregnancy was not developing as normal. Something was wrong with the baby…with me. They were given the option to end my life, before it had even begun.

Some part of my parents knew that both they and I could handle whatever life was going to throw my way. They sat down to a cup of tea, and after much discussion, they decided that *God makes no mistakes*. They followed their instincts and faith, knowing that I was meant to enter this world.

I was born with visual impairment and chronic juvenile rheumatoid arthritis. While overjoyed with my arrival, my parents questioned whether I would ever see beyond a life of struggle.

Gaining In-sight

The first five years of my life were spent in and out of hospital. The effects of the chronic rheumatoid arthritis flare-ups left me constantly in pain, during a time and in a place where the medical community was not equipped with the resources they have today. The doctors had never seen someone so young in such anguish, and they didn't really know how to help me.

My memories of hospitalization date back to just before I turned two. I recall receiving countless needles from the nuns who were the nurses in charge of my care. I also recall going into what I termed *Louise's world* during treatments. At a very young age, I learned to go within myself, to a happy place, in order to create positive memories. From that space, I trusted that the doctors would know how to alleviate my pain, and that my parents would always be instinctive aware of when I needed care.

I grew up very fast and learned from the adults who surrounded me every day in hospital. At two years of age, I could instinctively tell the nuns in the hospital whether or not I required a needle to ease my pain. Very early on, there was a determined quality to the decisions I made while faced with the effects of chronic juvenile rheumatoid arthritis and visual impairment. It was the in-sight I gained while in *Louise's world*.

My parents were the most wonderful and insightful people to have come in to this world with. When you're little, you don't understand everything. What I did know was that the pain I experienced during the arthritis flare-ups felt much like my bones were a face cloth that was being harshly rung out. It was hard to even eat being in that much agony. The doctors told my parents that I was too frail and was going to die. My mother, refusing to accept the medical prediction, had the idea of slipping little drops of wine on to my tongue to stimulate my appetite and allow me to eat and gain strength. I am forever grateful for my parent's wisdom, faith and sheer determination. It is beyond doubt that I gained my insight from my mother, and her little droplets of wine. They may have very well saved my life.

When the pain became fierce, I could easily have lost the strength to go on. Even at a very young age, I was resilient enough to defy medical odds. In spite of the sheer aching of my body, I felt empowered by my positive family environment. "Tomorrow will be better," my parents would always tell me. They also provided me with the greatest gift: never treating me as though I was any different than my brothers, or lacking of any ability.

My life growing up was vastly different than most children, never being physically able to go outside to play. When I did feel well enough to play, I made the very most of it. And when I didn't, I leapt into the playground of my imagination. It was my parents' creativity that spurred this determination. Once, while in hospital, they brought in a bright orange ride-on tractor. The steering wheel and tires were a deep black, which allowed me to vaguely see their shapes in contrast with the bright orange paneling. My parents intuitively knew how to help me gain mobility beyond the pain and restrictiveness of my condition, and that little tractor quickly gave me the ability to learn how to sit up and maneuver around. It also gave me a lot of freedom. My parents were soon chasing me through the hospital, as I learned how to ride down the hall and through the elevator doors on my tractor. Even at a very young age, I had a sense of adventure and risk-taking … and no physical limitations were going to hold me back from exploring what lay around the corner.

When I was two years old, my father, a traveling salesman, was away Monday to Friday. My mother did not drive. I questioned how Mum was going to get me out and about in the community. Trying to find someone to get me to the hospital three times a week for physiotherapy sessions presented a unique challenge. It also presented an opportunity for me to learn of my own insightfulness.

For a two-year old, I spoke very well. I understood much of what was being said around me. Knowing this, my father crafted a scenario to help find me a suitable hospital chauffeur. One day, he came home from work and announced that he would be having a tea party with some of his friends. He asked if I would like to join in. When the time came for our tea party, two friends of dad's came to the house. Physically unable to walk, I simply sat back and observed my father and his friends, happy to be a part of the occasion.

After a delightful evening of stories shared, it was time for our two guests to leave, and we all said our goodbyes. Dad immediately asked me which of his friends I liked best. I told him Michel was my favorite, as he had a gentle way about him, and kept looking at me and smiling at me throughout his visit.

To my surprise, my father had orchestrated the tea party as a means for me to personally select a suitable chauffeur to take me to and from the hospital. That was the first time that I can remember acknowledging and appreciating my instincts. I trusted the way I felt about Michel and the connection that I sensed with him. My father also trusted my instincts to make this important decision. In doing so, he helped develop my self-confidence and resilience at a very young age.

I had made a new partnership with Michel, and found means by which to explore the world … even if that world extended only as far as going from our house to the hospital. Still, I longed to be a traveling salesperson like my father when I grew up, so I could explore even greater opportunities.

Setting objectives early on in my life was tied to my theory that I would only be able to go after something I could actually *see* in my mind's eye. Being visually impaired, I quickly learned to *see beyond sight*. Setting objectives based on mental images and emotional strength drove me to defy the odds and become who I am today.

I have always balanced my successes with a healthy dose of reality. I knew that I was never going to be a pilot; however, that didn't mean that I wouldn't soar far above any limitations that the medical community and society at large had placed upon me as a young child. And so, when the doctors had told me that I would never walk, I chose to believe differently.

At the age of four, I spent my days at home with my mother. I would sit in my favorite rocking chair, close my eyes and go to the imaginative place within myself where I created possibility – also known as *Louise's world*. There, I would visualize myself walking. When my mother would go to the basement to do laundry, I would edge myself out of my rocking chair and test my legs, day after day. Some days I fell flat on the floor, causing her to run furiously upstairs in fear, but I persevered.

A few months later, my two brothers, parents and I were gathering for a regular family dinner. That night, I announced that I had something to show them. To their concern, I started moving as if I was going to get up out of my chair. Refusing offers of help form my shocked family members, I stood up and walked several steps, unassisted, and in defiance of all medical prognosis. I walked because I believed that I could – first inside of my mind, and then in reality. I translated my thoughts and beliefs into physical action. At four years of age, I had made the impossible possible… though I am not sure I could have found a way to articulate just how I did it.

My parents always encouraged me to do everything I put my mind to, and offered to develop and maximize the abilities that I did have. At the age of ten, I moved six hundred miles away from my family to attend school at an institute for the blind. There again, I learned to grow up very quickly.

At school, I met a group of people with whom I could so easily relate. We enjoyed one another's company and we learned together. I had become a part of a new family, as we all joined forces to overcome any of the challenges perceived to be tied to visual impairment. The program helped turn me into a more self-sufficient and determined individual. By the age of twelve, I could cook a full meal for twenty people on a tight budget, and I saw myself to be no different or no less able than anyone else I knew. I had become even more resilient.

My increased abilities carried me through two and a half years of university before my independence was swept away by a severe flare-up of my chronic rheumatoid arthritis. For an entire year, I was bedridden, and I spent six months relying on a wheelchair to regain my mobility. It was a time that was hugely challenging to my spirit and all that I wanted to be, do and have. It also became a time of even greater insight.

Being restricted to a wheelchair and trying to access places in the community gave me a broader picture of just how limited our world can be to those with disabilities. Then and there, I knew that I would, and had to, become a voice for disability awareness and etiquette. I also had visions of a budding career that would support my vision. When the flare-up subsided, I dedicated myself to my ambition of growing into managerial positions in the non-profit sector.

I continued to focus on my career for most of my twenties – a time I fondly refer to as *my roaring twenties*. During those years, I had some great fun and personal triumphs. I purchased my very own Buick Park Avenue at the age of twenty-five. Given that I was visually impaired, no one had wanted to give me the keys to their car, so I went out and bought my own. I would drive the car around the mall parking lots when the stores were closed on Sundays. My passengers would alert me when I was getting close to buildings and other vehicles to help me avoid potentially crashing.

Every day, my world was opening up even more. I even dated occasionally, though never felt as though I had met my soul mate…until I turned thirty. It was then that I met the love of my life, Stephen. Three years later, we were planning to get married.

The same year as our planned marriage, we were in a horrible car crash. I was in the passenger seat when we were hit by a car that did not yield at a stop sign. Our car swerved out of control and slammed into a giant tree, crushing the front of the car directly on top of me. Two months before our wedding day, I was hauled from the car by the jaws-of-life. In spite of yet another hit in my life, Stephen and I married as planned. It took me the first five years of our life together to physically recover from the accident.

The accident was a hit that changed my life as I knew it. It provided real time for introspection. Once again, I had been given a second chance at life, and a chance to sit back and ask what it was that I truly wanted to do. During my recovery, I wrote two lists: one of what I *could* do, and the other what I *liked* to do. At the top of both lists was talking. I knew that because my tongue and my brain were muscles, they would not be affected by the accident, or my chronic rheumatoid arthritis. That was when I began my journey to becoming a professional speaker, while continuously adjusting my life around the pain and low energy that came as part and parcel of the crash and the ongoing effects of rheumatoid arthritis.

One of the new medications prescribed to ease my pain during that time presented a challenge all new to me. The specialist told me that this medication would affect my weakest organ. I knew then I would lose the rest of my sight.

Upon hearing the news, I barely ate and didn't socialize with anyone for two weeks. I thought my life was over. However, it didn't take long for me to sit myself down and think, *Louise, you know this is going to happen. What are you going to do about it?* I had been resilient through so many physical challenges, why should this have been any different?

My colleagues offered the helpful suggestion that I blindfold myself and begin learning the skills of walking with a white cane, reading braille and re-learning to cook safely. Following their suggestion, I prepared for my inevitable fate. For an entire year, I planned ahead for going completely blind.

When the day came that I woke up, put on my glasses, and could not see, I knew that it had finally happened. And so, I picked up my white cane and walked to work, following the route that I had learned while blind-folded. I remember feeling the warmth of the sun beat down on my face that day, and I knew that everything would turn out alright. No feat was too big for me to overcome. Coping with illness and visual impairment as part of everyday life for me early on had opened the gateway to a life of in-sight and resilience. Give me *the impossible*, and I'll show you the pos-sibility within. Every hit soon became an opportunity to unveil a new gift.

Sharing Insight

I became the person I am today because I had a world of possibility shown to me at a very young age. Every experience of my childhood has shaped me, and has led to greater awareness of what potential we all have. As I grew to respect myself, I realized I had to educate people how to respect me for who I am. And respect for me came to include accep-tance and respect for my partner in crime.

Somewhere along the ribbon of my life, I was introduced to the idea that a guide dog would increase my independence and introduce endless pos-sibilities into my world. Since 1996, I have been using guide dogs from the MIRA Foundation. I am currently the proud team leader of a four-legged black beauty named Cadillac. He is with me when I lead train-ing sessions, attend conferences and give keynote speeches. When I fly across the country or travel locally, I find I must regularly educate others on respect, etiquette and awareness. Upon boarding a plane, I often have to reassure people that the dog will be quiet and well-behaved and ensure that there is sufficient room for the dog in front of my feet.

Over the years, I have found myself faced with people who showed a lack of understanding and respect for the fact that being blind means that my eyes have four legs and need to be by my side at all times…even if I am tens of thousands of feet in the air. While it takes time, I am usually able to help the airline and hotel staff understand our needs and abilities when I have my guide dog by my side. These are the occasions that further fuel my mission to educate others on how to approach those of us who live with physical challenges. Some days it requires only awareness, and at other times some negotiation and flexibility.

Through all the hours in the hospital as a child, the time I spent working in management in the non-profit sector, and the travelling cross-country as a speaker and trainer, I have learned that team work is the single most important factor in helping us all unleash our full potential. That is precisely why I now dedicate my days to helping individuals and organizations gain awareness of each other's needs and effectively communicate their objectives. My life-long passion has culminated in showing others just what is possible when they put their minds to it. We shape our worlds by how we think. We allow our eyes to often guide us before our instincts, when we can live doing just the opposite. I am a walking testimonial of this fact, being able to see the possibility within others *because* I cannot physically see.

Though the gifts of my hits have been plentiful, my ultimate gift is being able to help others gain insights into making *the impossible possible* in every aspect of their lives. I have created and realized my dream of using my brain and my tongue. I now make a living as a professional speaker, traveling the country helping others, just as my father did. I am the traveling saleswoman, carrying a briefcase of possibility with me everywhere I go.

I am forever grateful for everything my parents taught me I could do. Thanks Mum and Dad.

About Louise

BIO:

Louise Levesque-Burley is a self-motivated, energetic, dynamic individual who uses the lessons of her own life to lead others to leave their fears behind and move forward boldly toward fulfilling their goals. She is proudly the first blind Canadian to graduate with a Diploma in Adult Education from Saint Francis Xavier University, Past President of the Canadian Association of Professional Speakers (CAPS) Atlantic, and a member of the Certified Coaches Federation of Canada. She is also the author of *Through my Eyes – INsights into Disability Etiquette.*

Drawing on many years of senior management experience in the not-for-profit sector, Louise offers a unique approach to personal and professional development. She has immersed herself in a life of *making the impossible possible* and using her leadership skills to educate and inspire.

Despite her physical challenges, she maintains an active and healthy lifestyle: traveling, wine-tasting, dancing, walking on the beach and enjoying the sounds of nature.

Website: www.shared-vision.ca

Louise Levesque-Burley and her guide dog

Topher Wurts

HIT:

Like most new parents, Topher and Jana upheld hopes and dreams for a typically successful life for their son...until he was diagnosed as classically autistic and their future imaginary child died.

GIFT:

Freed of the weight of living up to expectations, Topher and his family discovered how every precious moment is fresh with abundant opportunities to celebrate authentic success and cherish individuality.

Letting Go
of the Imaginary Child
– *TOPHER WURTS*

To say that life was hectic when our second son, Kirby, was born just eleven months after our first son, Zandy, would have been an understatement. My wife, Jana, and I were raising *Irish Twins* – two kids less than a year apart. Zandy seemed to be a normal enough child. He was gregarious and typical in every respect. He made eye contact, pointed at things, and interacted. He was always exploring, and was quick to crawl and then walk. We took him everywhere and he didn't seem to mind. When Kirby came along eleven months later, he too seemed typical.

The boys were energetic and happy. When Kirby was a little older, they shared a room and their cribs were across from one another. Kirby was a bit quirky as a baby. He didn't sleep as much as his older brother Zandy. Actually, he didn't really sleep much at all. He was fussier and harder to get to nap. He would throw everything out of his crib and stay up for hours. Zandy didn't seem to mind though; he just slept through it.

Kirby has piercing blue eyes and would often busy himself at things that only he seemed to understand. We knew that Kirby interacted differently and seemed to prefer his own company a bit. However, he was healthy and was happy enough, so we didn't think anything of it.

While I worked long days and traveled extensively in my role with Reuters, Jana was trying to keep it all together raising two young boys, while dealing with chronic illness. To be frank, Jana was struggling a bit and finding those early days with the babies to be physically and emotionally stressful. For me, it felt like the perfect storm. I was wrestling with understanding, helping, and caring for both Jana and the boys, while trying to manage a demanding out-of-town job. We knew that we needed help, and therefore decided to look into an au pair – hosting a foreign worker who could assist us with Zandy and Kirby.

Our initial question was where to begin our search, and what countries to look into recruiting from. We talked about it and decided everyone we'd ever met from New Zealand were cool and hip. With the help of Google, we located an au pair agency out of New Zealand that had a young lady named Nikki who wanted to try out a stint in the United States. It wasn't long thereafter that Nikki arrived at our home in Philadelphia.

Nikki was from Blenheim, New Zealand – a very small town in wine country on the South Island. She'd never been far from home, though she and few friends decided to come to the States to be au pairs. What they couldn't have known was how far from each other they'd be while working in the USA. We knew it was hard for her to be far from home and friends, though Nikki was one of the few who didn't turn back. She was dedicated to our family.

Kind and lovely, Nikki had worked in a preschool back home and was truly great with the kids. Having grown up working with her parents on their farm and in a mussel farm business, she was undaunted by anything. She could drive tractors, boats, and everything in between. She was a very resourceful young lady. She fit right in at our place.

To help make her feel at home, we got her a free New Zealand calling plan, a Mac laptop, and internet access to stay in touch with her parents and friends back home, and a television channel that allowed her to follow the New Zealand All Blacks Rugby Team. She taught us about rugby, and we taught her about American football. We knew Nikki was a long way from home and wanted to do our best to make her feel comfortable with connections and reminders of her small town on the South Island.

When Nikki had first arrived, we could barely understand her heavy New Zealand accent, though before long we got it, she found that her homesickness became bearable, and she became one of the gang. She got along seamlessly with all of our friends and extended family, joining us on all of our adventures.

Nikki and Jana quickly became a team and got along quite well. Part friend and part elder, Jana helped Nikki to acclimate to being far from home. She helped her explore and do many wonderful things during her time in the States. Nikki was very competent and independent, and could do anything with the boys. We trusted her wholeheartedly, which even allowed Jana and I to get away alone now and again. Nikki bonded with the boys and they with her. In no time at all, she had become a second mom and a big sister, and a part of our family. Nikki, Jana, and the boys went on plenty of adventures and did all kinds of activities.

Nikki was always joyful and easy-going, catching us somewhat by surprise the day she wanted to talk to us about something serious.

With some hesitation, she said, "Kirby seems like he might be autistic."

As it turns out, she had been warming up to the idea for some time, and had even sought input from our close friends. Our friends all encouraged her to just to say what she thought. While we were surprised, we kept an open mind, feeling as though it was better to be open-minded than miss something important. That is what I tell other parents to be who are in the early stages of diagnosis.

Nikki explained how some of Kirby's behaviors were similar to kids with autism in the preschool where she worked back home in New Zealand. Based on her insight, we started to pay more attention to Kirby's behaviors. At the time, he was only eighteen months old, making it difficult to see his actions as so different than normal.

Nikki had seen it and she nailed it. While her perspective was initially very unappealing to hear, we weren't going to ignore her. In the end, Nikki likely saved us months or even years of lost intervention time by being brave enough to come and talk to us that day. Jana and I were grateful for her openness, and for our dear friends who allowed her to feel comfortable in approaching us to bring it to our attention.

My advice to all parents in the early stages of diagnoses: be brave and be open minded. Don't waste precious time.

The hardest thing about an autism diagnosis, or any special needs diagnosis, at the birth or first few months of life of one's child, is that it's like a death. The diagnosis comes and it floors you. It feels like the death of a close friend or family member.

Why is this? I think it's because each of us, upon hearing we're expecting, constructs an imaginary future child. Before we come into this world, our parents already have our imaginary future all figured out. We're going to be doctors, scientists, academics, artists, musicians, statesmen, entrepreneurs, or whatever… and we're going to be really good at it. We'll be the most successful of the lot. Our future's so bright that we'll have to wear shades. However, this isn't feasible, and we all know it. At some level, our parents know it too, but wanting the best is human nature none the less.

Over the next twenty or thirty years, we go through life killing off that 'future child' in a death by a thousand cuts. Over two decades, one small piece at a time, our parents are disenfranchised of their imaginary future version of us. And in the end, with the imaginary future jettisoned, our parents come to peace with who we've become, who we are, and the reality of their child's future.

The special needs parent is not given such a luxury of time to come to terms with the death of their imaginary future child. In a sentence, with the stroke of a pen, an expert declares that their child is not ever going to be anything like imagined. This child has special needs, a handicap or a disability, and the parent is hit with the realization, in that moment, that their imaginary future child is dead.

It's crippling. It's immediate. It's incontrovertible. It's irreversible. It's unfathomable.

In this pivotal moment, parents seem to go one of three ways. Some parents fall into the abyss of grief and never quite recover. They drift in an endless sadness, seemingly forever. Some parents are angry, going on a mission to determine why and how this happened to them. They are focused on a cure and are committed to resuscitating their imaginary future child at any cost. And then some parents decide to move on, accepting the death of the imaginary future child. For whatever reason, they decide to accept their special needs baby just as he or she is. They commit to advocating, nurturing, running interventions, and creating a life and a future for this child in ways they can realistically manage.

After heeding Nikki's insight, we began to observe Kirby a little more closely. We discussed and we debated with friends as to whether Kirby did in fact have autism, and how we should proceed. We started to find folks with experience in autism, and we spent hours searching the internet for resources. We learned about common behaviors, such as perseverating on repetitive activities, hand flapping, lack of eye contact, and others. Nikki was a great resource through it all. She was the only one of us who had any real world experience with autism.

About that time, I had lunch with a close colleague in New York. He gave me the most wonderful advice. He said, "There is no danger in an over-diagnosis. The worst case is the kid gets a lot of extra attention. However, the opportunity lost by putting off starting the hard work of creating an intervention that will help an autism child to thrive is immeasurable. That time will never come back. The lost opportunity is immense. Do not fret an autism diagnosis. It's better to have to revise to a lesser diagnosis than to lose time."

He was right. We immediately called the local Easter Seals office, which offered autism diagnosing and coordinated pre-school age intervention programs. Within a couple of weeks, they sent a nice lady named Anne to our home. She observed Kirby's every word and action, taking notes and gathering some light data. A few days later, she returned to confirm that Kirby had autism. And yet, we still pushed to make sure.

The diagnosis didn't seem very scientific and was not quantitative. There's no baseline to measure against. It's not like a disease, where one can state whether you're sick or you're not. Unlike an illness, this wasn't a case of there being a treatment or not. The diagnosis came from a lot of observations and finished with the exclamation point that this wasn't a curable thing; it was about a child with a fundamentally different brain. The best treatment was using various behavioral and other interventions, depending on your specific case, to help the child to improve.

We had Anne come back, but the diagnosis remained the same. I continued to push back. Every parent has some denial. It's about whether you choose to get past that. Kirby wasn't so obviously different to us at his young age, and we wanted to believe that he had a future. It felt like the five phases of grief. Parents in our situation can so easily experience denial, anger, bargaining, depression, and finally acceptance; and many parents get stuck in one phase or another.

Anne told us something that I'll never forget. She said, "I know this is going to sound unbelievable, but I've been working with very young autistic kids a long time, and I can pretty much just look at a child and tell you if they're autistic."

She was right, I definitely didn't like it. I preferred data, baselines, and measurements. I'm a software and science kind of guy. Eleven years later, I now know what she meant. I can do it too: look and identify people with autism. It's weird, but true. I believe her now. I know Nikki could see it too.

As we dove into research and sought the assistance of autism experts, we discovered that there are many types of interventions, such as Applied Behavior Analyses (see http://researchautism.net/autism-interventions/types). We studied and assessed most of the intervention methods and determined that our work with Kirby would involve a lot of trial and error. We decided to use a mix and match approach to create a program that worked for us. We didn't want to fully dive into one sole program and become committed to only that one type. That approach seemed too risky.

We were so lucky for Nikki's insight. Kirby's services and our intervention work started when he was just over eighteen months old. We had an early autism diagnosis, which meant that services were justified all the way onward from those early days. This meant less fighting with schools and the state. We also learned how to be strong advocates. Through thick and thin, we searched out skilled interventionists. We faced many trials and tribulations of various requirements, and dealt with Kirby's various behaviors, particularly his pension for running away.

We made the conscious choice to continue accepting the death of an imaginary future child, and something wonderful happened. We saw Kirby with clarity, and without filters or judgement. Every day and every development became cause for celebration. Instead of a living a life of disappointment for the next twenty years, wanting to Kirby to be something or someone other than who he was, we, the accepting parents, were given the gift of daily celebration. The same holds true for any parents of autistic children who are willing to accept the death of an imaginary future child.

The road of coping with the daily trials of autism is harder than ignorance or denial in many ways. There are countless small, practical problems that litter the way, attempting to trip and snag any progress or understanding you achieve. However, without the burden of the imaginary future, a life of celebration is opened up each and every day. That is the gift of autism.

Nowadays, Kirby keeps coming out of his shell, slowly but surely. He keeps learning. He's physically healthy and happy. He loves all things sensory and taught himself to swim at a very young age. He generally likes to jump, swing, swim, and burrow in the sand. He loves hats and is often seen sporting a stack of them. His intelligence jumps out in different ways. We've watched him learn to copy words from *Thomas The Tank Engine* books and CDs into his iPad to search out videos and images of Thomas. Now in seventh grade, he is starting to read on his own and he can do basic math. He loves watching Thomas videos and he seems to have the map to the YouTube videos memorized. He's adept at using the web browser and other iPad apps. He follows instructions and helps with all kinds of chores and activities at our direction. He's even got his own video on YouTube: https://youtu.be/2gNSiofMIdM

Jana and I realize that so many others have so much more to contend with than we do. There are times that continue to test us though. Kirby is always challenging us to keep him safe. He frequently runs away and has little safety awareness. Sometimes his creativity can also cause challenges – for example, he took all the flour from the pantry and made the master bedroom look like the movie *Frozen* by spreading and shaking flour all over everything to look like snow. His experiences and behaviors have become part of my blog at http://about.autismvillage.com/blogs/main/.

Being parents of a child on the autism spectrum is incredibly taxing. Forty-seven percent of couples divorce before their child with autism is five, and sixty-eight percent before the child is eight. Jana and I are sticking it out, but it can be really hard. Kirby's diagnosis has made our relationship stronger in some ways. We regularly have to 'tag one another out,' because patience isn't endless. It's scary too. When Kirby runs off, we never know if he'll come back safely. Those times are very stressful. It's also difficult to ensure that we save time for and don't unduly burden Zandy. Like all autism parents, we're perennially tired and overwhelmed with paperwork, research, and the daily chores that come with a child on the autism spectrum.

We don't know where Kirby will go, or how he and we will get there. The truth is, we don't care. We try hard every day, and we focus on what is practical. We keep our perspective on what is possible, and we celebrate our accomplishments. All of us celebrate our accomplishments. Through all of our research of interventions and support, the best results came from letting go of the *why, how, what did I do or not do,* and *how do I cure this* of it all. They come from acceptance and focus on celebrating daily success.

The imaginary future child was just that, imaginary. He could never replace the wonderful, quirky, happy, explorer that is Kirby.

About Topher

BIO:

Topher Wurts has been around the block a few times in the world of business, where he was known for bringing together marketing, technology and teamwork. After learning his son Kirby had autism, he was floored. He and his family had become one of 2.8 million families in the U.S. who have been affected by autism. Putting his entrepreneurial hat on, he invented Autism Village.

Autism Village sets itself apart as unique from the myriad of educational apps on the internet for autism parents. The organization produces apps which are especially designed to be useful for managing the practical challenges of life with autism, based on the needs of the community of autism 'Villagers.' Topher conceived the idea of Autism Village as an initiative to produce practical, useful, and helpful management tools and services for those living life on the autism spectrum. The goal? To improve the future for millions with autism.

Website: www.autismvillage.com

Kirby Wurts and his brother Zandy

Dena Churchill

HIT:

Dena's life was torn in to a hundred little pieces by a tumultuous divorce that ensued after the parting was chaperoned by the police. Her chiropractic practice, family home, custody of her kids and ability to re-pay debt lay scattered before her for dissection.

GIFT:

Showcasing the divinity of divorce as a wonderful world of joy beyond pain and suffering, Dena now shares her strength as an international speaker, author, chiropractor and mind-body health coach.

Ripening into Gratitude
– DENA CHURCHILL

On July 11, 1997, the guests arrived wearing ties, shined shoes, pressed white shirts, flowing shirts and dresses in linen, lace, silks and other fine fabrics. Faint scents of perfume and cologne defined the space of kisses and warm congratulation embraces. The room at a private country fishing club on the lake was adorned with copious candles and glass vases of purple, pink and white lupines picked that morning. Through the wall of glass was a shimmering sun-lit lake surrounded by a lush green background of trees and grasses that added a further element of the natural beauty of light, love and divinity to the day. It was a rather traditional wedding service with a quiet air of reflection. My fiancé and I had gathered to announce our commitment to each other, pledging to be together in sickness and health, for richer or poorer, until death do us part.

The next five years were filled with a freedom of advancing our professional careers woven into our adventures of rock climbing, kayaking and baby-making. The memories made were those that I have cherished. Amidst the lingerie, breast-milk, and my patient files, was a purposeful place as a wife, mother and chiropractic doctor. And then, it happened – a shift in awareness. There was a calling for me to expand and stretch a little more.

I believe evolution sets things up this way: the universe would like us to focus on supporting ourselves and then creating and nurturing our next generation. The evolutionary intention continues as we grow. We grow ourselves, our family, our community and our country, then we step out into the world and beyond. Some will grow together with their partner and families, and some will need to create space for further growth. When unrest and communication issues arose in my marriage, I turned to personal development seminars…and stepped into the realization that I was one who would need to create space for further growth.

The likely turning point in my marriage and life was the day I shared my sacred 150-word life purpose with my husband and he didn't understand it. Personal development courses had inspired clarity of who I am and what I was accomplishing on earth. My purpose was something I had always known inside, but never talked about. When I finally mustered the courage to share my soul's song, I felt as though he couldn't hear it. To have him mock the purpose of what I felt called to do was a painful reminder of us growing apart.

As I began to shift my perception into one of worldly service, there was less attention on family matters, in particular my relationship with my husband. September 2006, I was given the ultimatum to change, or he was leaving the marriage.

In the early morning hours of many autumn nights, thoughts and dreams pierced my mind. I couldn't hear myself think. My options were to stay in a marriage and change to meet my husband's wishes, or leave him and answer my new calling. The back and forth debate produced a pounding in my head and an aching in my heart.

When the fruit is ripe, it knows when to fall from the tree. On December 26, 2006, as I lay in a cold bed my heart is racing, my mind jumping from one thought to another, my stomach burning with fear, and a lump in my throat too big to swallow, I asked my husband for a divorce. Suddenly, all of the background noise of outer voices increased to the point of being almost deafening. I could hear the voices of family responsibility, including my husband and children's, begging and pleading for me to reconsider for fear of what damage my decision would do to our family. Amongst the tears, fears and chorus of forbidden choices, I knew that I had a new path, however, I didn't yet know where it was leading.

How did I know it was time to move on? If you are asking the question and there is doubt, you are not ready. Pain pushes us until our purpose pulls us … and mine was woven into the fibers of my heart.

Over the next few months, divorce and separation played into the regular mix of family, friends, finances, fitness and maintaining my mental faculties. Emotions were running wild. A separation agreement that once seemed flawless escalated to a police escort and intervention. The weirdest fears and nightmares began to tax my already weighty thoughts. I worried about my two boys, then nine and five years of age. Where would they live? I wondered if I would find another partner at thirty-five. Had I made a mistake? The questions began to mount. Would this decision ruin me financially? Was my choice stemming from a selfish perspective? Is my husband asking himself these same questions?

As my mind was caught in a vortex of unanswered questions, I progressed through the stages of grief (as per Kubler-Ross):

- Denial (this isn't *happening* to me!)

- Anger (why is this happening to *me?*)

- Bargaining (I promise I'll be a better person *if…*)

- Depression (I don't *care* anymore)

- Acceptance (*I'm ready* for whatever comes)

- At about the same time in my quandary, I discovered the *Demartini Method* by Dr. John Demartini – a tool that I found instrumental in showing a neutral place of seeing both mine and my husband's perspectives. The method had me do work such as taking inventory of my former spouse's qualities that I liked, and those I didn't. The ones I liked was very short and emotionally charged. Then, I took a hard look inside, and at Dr. Demartini's suggestion, I looked at the traits in myself that were the same as those I disliked in my spouse. In the end, I saw that, I was all that I disliked in my former spouse but maybe in a different form. We were reflections of one another. The traits that I was denying most in myself were the ones to which I was most critical of in him.

As I progressed through Dr. Demartini's seminar, I was asked to see that some of my former husband's family, friends, our neighbors and his co-workers and staff described him in the exact opposite way as I did. Just the same, there were others equal in magnitude that would describe me differently than I saw myself. At that point in the seminar, I felt my body relax, as a lump appeared in my throat. I was literally trying to swallow the fact that what I had believed as truths were really my own labels and judgments seen through my limited perspective. Naturally, those that shared my values agreed with me, and those that share my former spouse's values would agree with him. I could clearly see that life is our perception, and the color of the picture depends on which glasses we are wearing.

Moving through the process, I then worked on seeing how the traits I had labeled as negative have a benefit, and how positive traits can actually do a disservice. How can yelling at someone be beneficial? How does lying serve us? When initially asked to visit these thoughts, I found myself feeling quite aggravated, as if my beliefs and thoughts were being questioned. I was beginning to resent this Demartini dude. He didn't know my husband; so how can he be asking me to see the benefit in something that everyone knows is disgraceful behavior? At one point, I found myself ready to storm out of the seminar. I didn't care what anyone else thought. As my thoughts raced back and forth from staying to leaving, I moved a little further in my mind to imagine what I would feel like after leaving. Would I still be angry? The answer was *yes*. In fact, I'd likely be even more angry, because I had paid $1000 in advance for the seminar and was without the "aha" moment I was hoping to experience! My desire was to release my own anger…and not lose the money I had invested in this process. I stayed glued to my seat that day, and sat with the uncomfortable nature of the fear that John Demartini could embarrass me. In between reciting a number of swear words to myself, I kept looking for the answer.

As I struggled through the workbook, doubted the process, and fought against Dr. Demartini's method, I found some grace when he said, "If challenge makes us stronger, support only sustains us which is more loving challenge or support?" As I scanned the past memories of all the events I had labeled challenging, I could see that they did indeed bring growth in strength, confidence and resourcefulness that otherwise I would not have experienced. Could it be that love is both the support and challenge?

During the course of the seminars, we were also asked to realize that there is an equal and opposite force present synchronously in time and space, or what Dr. Demartini called the GOD principle (grand organized design) – an intelligence in the universe that keeps all in a balance. I tried to isolate a moment in my memory when my spouse was being critical of me and to ask myself who was being supportive? I could see it with greater clarity than ever before: my family and friends jumped into support me when I was being challenged. I could even feel their unspoken support when they were not present in the physical space of the challenger. There was always someone supportive available; if not my parents, then a co-worker, best friend or counsellor. With each example I worked through, I could see a loving matrix that always has given me *both* support and challenge. At the moment my former spouse is criticizing me, someone is praising me. At the moment someone else is challenging me, my former spouse often came to my rescue. In fact, because of the challenges I faced in my marriage, I was brought support from family and friends I hadn't connected with in years. Even my very first boyfriend even appeared out of the past to offer love and advice! It is amazing to see how one relationship can be dissolving and another reappearing simultaneously. New relationships emerge to balance the marriage that we are transforming. No longer was I afraid to look at my life, and deep within myself.

Only through the challenges with my former spouse and the choice to divorce had I gained a strength and certainty of my values and purpose, found new relationships to bring me new lessons, and discovered a resourcefulness and belief in myself. I could see how things were perfect as they were. Had my former spouse acted in any other way, he would have done me a disservice. I found myself in a place of moving beyond the verse of the "I forgive you" tune, into a chorus of true love that sounded more like, "Thank you for this style of love and learning, for it is in the midst of the mine/mind field I have found my own diamond."

When we reach a point of gratitude, and can say and feel the true sentiment of the words "Thank you. I love you. I would not change you," then our work is complete and we have empowered our life with this divine experience.

At the onset of my separation, I had called Dr. Demartini with the question of how to get through a divorce with love and gratitude. I had thought there would be a magic phrase, recommendation or solution. It took me years to understand that the answers were inside of me all along. I just had to get out of my own way to see them. In the end, the liberation from my marriage was worth the four lives it affected.

Dr. John Demartini is a visionary in creating this noble prize worthy methodology to finding divine order in what appears to be chaos. He was instrumental in helping me find order in the great intricacies and challenges of the major life change that is divorce.

G.W. Leibniz said, "If we could understand the order of the universe well enough, we would find that it surpasses all the wishes of the wisest and that it is impossible to make it better than it is."

The universe brings together complimentary opposites; this unity of two sides is true love. We move through our lessons of love to gain more clarity through reflection. It is, however, never an easy process to question what we've created for ourselves and dig deep within pain to help answers surface. The reward is what makes all of the hurt worthwhile, and that reward is the discovery that we are all one in spirit. Even when we feel emotional anguish and hatred toward another, as I initially had toward my former spouse, we can balance the positive and negative emotions to find love. That which we can't love, we will attract…until such point that we can love the entirety of who we are – the good and bad, light and dark, the oneness with all that is.

The ultimate goal is to love all the parts of ourselves: the selfish and the selfless, the giver and the taker, the cruel and the kind. Those you meet in this lifetime and who love you, as a spouse does, may appear different to you. I have learned that opposites do attract. If two people are the same, one is redundant. Differences are what draw us together with the purpose of love, and love is the ultimate goal and the way of the new consciousness. We are building an understanding that we are simply pure love and light; and shadows and dark hues may simply be a function and property of that light. Times of struggle and challenge are necessary, strengthening and bringing clarity to our loving light. It is like blowing on a fire to increase the flame. Our journey in a life of contrasts is simply bringing us home to the understanding that we have the potential to be and overcome anything.

With divorce comes new support and challenges, some in familiar forms, and others fully foreign. I am grateful to have many of my challenges. For some, challenge may come through divorce, for others it may come in another form, such as a friend's divorce, a family illness, a financial crisis, etc., and for others, there may be a stream of challenges that begin with divorce. What is critical is that we take the time to do the work to transform loss or pain into love. That is our best reassurance of reducing the sting of the chaos. There is always going to be a pile of fecal material to balance a pleasant life, but we get to choose our corner.

Before my divorce, I was questioning God. How could he put me in such a situation? What was I to learn? I was ready to leave my husband full of fear, anger and resentment. To dissolve my guilt about destroying my husband and our family, I had to see how it would serve him and them to have me leave. Once I could see the benefits and opportunity for all of us, I had the confidence to move. I knew in that moment that the challenge of the divorce would empower our family to greater heights of strength, confidence and love. Before I could leave my marriage, I had to come to truly love and be grateful for it. And then, I questioned if even in my leaving, had I even in fact *lost*? Do you ever really leave or lose anything or is it woven into your heart matrix? Laws of thermodynamics says that energy is conserved through space and time so that there are no losses or gains, just transformations. My studies of Dr. Demartini's work confirmed so. He says, "The masses live in this world of gains and losses; the masters live in a world of transformation."

Since working the Demartini Method, I have seen that the traits I considered most challenging I can now see and feel were my greatest teachers. Addicted to the peace and pleasure of love and the healing and construction of the body and the world, I attracted a combat system engineer in a husband to teach me the balance. As I learn to love all parts of myself, I could see my former spouse as one of my greatest teachers of all parts of love, in and out of the marriage. His challenge and questioning of my purpose was to test my commitment. I dedicated my book and the spark of my learning to him.

There remain daily challenges and emotions that rise and fall with the tides. There are still issues with the kids that we don't always agree upon, but I now have the tools to find wisdom in the wall, certain of the perfection in every moment. Even the wisest of the wise still have emotions to work through, in fact E-motion or energy in motion is what stirs passion and excitement for life. Finding the gift within the hit balances our perceptions and brings us to a place of love and grace. If we look at each new challenge as a universal test and ask ourselves what love lesson we've gathered from the experience, we get promoted to our next series of tests. The learning and testing never stops. The hits are gifts turned upside down, so remember to turn your present bow side up!

Today, because of this challenge, I am stretched to expand into a global service, feeling called to share what I have learned with others. The divorce gave me the confidence to push past other barriers and just enough desperation to fuel new desires. I have been inspired to become a facilitator in the Demartini Method, author of my own book, *Divinity in Divorce: Power in Gratitude and Love* and a co-author of several other works. I now see myself not just as a local chiropractor, but as an innovator in women's empowerment in health and wellness. As an international speaker, author, chiropractor and a mind-body health coach, I am giving my service to the world. My next book explores universal truths and untruths that keep our world captive. In essence, it is about divorcing that which does not resonate with you in a much larger arena.

I like to think there are two things that move us: pain and inspiration. The divorce journey gave me both.

About Dena

BIO:

Dr. Dena Churchill is an international speaker, best-selling author, and innovator of women's empowerment in health and wellness. She is known for her ability to deeply connect with audiences through clarity, wisdom and humor. With a humble confidence, she draws on a wealth of real-life experiences to help you *Envision and Achieve Your Best*, in a way that is both entertaining and informative. Her purpose is to help mothers keep themselves and their families healthy, their work inspired, and their feminine powerful. She is the author of the book entitled, *Divinity in Divorce* and Co-author of *Pearls of Wisdom; Pure and Powerful* and the Amazon best-seller: *The Thought That Changed Your Life Forever.* Dena is a fan of yoga and loves to Latin dance. If you can't catch her in the chiropractic clinic or on the dance floor, you can find her online.

Websites: www.oxfordchiro.ca
www.drsexymom.com

Dr. Dena Churchill

Mark Black

HIT:

On a sunny May day, at the young age of twenty-three, Mark was told that without a new heart and two new lungs he would be dead before his twenty-fifth birthday.

GIFT:

With the acceptance of his newly transplanted organs, Mark chose to live from the heart and synthesize the lessons of his death-defying experience into speaking, writing and coaching endeavors as an Adversity Advisor to thousands across North America.

Perspective and Prioritization
– *MARK BLACK*

There are moments that are so powerful, so impactful on your life, that you can't fully grasp them as they happen. No matter how hard you try to take it all in, you simply can't process all of the information and emotion. So, you do your best to take in what you can, and then, as time passes, the rest begins to register. That is how I experienced the moment that forever changed my life.

At first it didn't even seem real. It was May, 2001. As I sat in the hospital exam room waiting to be seen, I knew that no matter what the doctor was going to tell me, my world was about to change. I just wasn't sure how much or in what way.

For twenty-three years, I had battled congenital heart disease. Actually, 'battled' is a strange word to use, because it didn't really feel like a fight to me. I was born with my condition. I had open-heart surgery the day I was born and another one on my first birthday. I knew nothing different. I dealt with many limitations, took a lot of medication, had frequent doctor visits, and endured painful testing throughout my youth, but it rarely never occurred to me that this was abnormal. I was six years old before I realized that everyone didn't have a big scar going down their chests.

My childhood was a game of balance. With the encouragement of my parents, I stretched my limits, continually walking a fine line between living a normal life and respecting the limitations of my heart problem. Most of the time, I walked that line effectively; but when I crossed it, the consequences were swift and severe. Hospitalizations were not a rarity for me, as my desire to push the limits sometimes landed me in dangerous and life-threatening situations.

There was the time I ran for the school bus and ended up unconscious in a snowbank. I awoke a few moments later to find my parents rushing down the street. Another time, I attempted to jump over a railing, caught my toe and landed me flat on my face, having fallen from four feet off the ground. I went into cardiac arrest and awoke to find my father leaning over me, pale-faced and panic-stricken, holding back tears as he did CPR. Then in May 2001, the proverbial straw broke the camel's back. This time there was no critical incident. It was more like a slow progression – a series of seemingly minor events that culminated in this pivotal moment.

In the early spring of that year I began to notice that something wasn't quite right. As I walked to school each day, I took note of my being short of breath more often. The hill I climbed to class felt as though it was steeper with each passing day. I felt more tired, had difficulty concentrating, and was losing weight.

To this day, I don't know what blinded me to what was happening. It may have been the gradual nature of the changes, the fact that I was a busy college student, or my immaturity and stubbornness. Whatever the case, I had ignored the obvious clues of what was coming, and I did so for far too long. I found myself sitting in a waiting room waiting for a doctor to tell me how the next part of my life would unfold.

After what seemed like hours, cardiologist Dr. Howlett finally came into the room. I could tell by the expression on his face that the news he was about to share wasn't good. Normally a jovial, energetic, character, Dr. Howlett entered the room that day grim-faced and somber. It was clear from that this meeting would be different than the dozens that preceded it. He walked over to where I was sitting with my parents and sat down. He had my thick medical file clutched in his hands – the compilation of years of work trying to keep my heart functional enough to keep me alive.

Finally, he looked at me and began to speak. "We've looked at all of the test results," he said. "You are in right and left-sided heart failure now. We have done everything we can with medications and non-invasive therapies. There is nothing more we can do here."

The words washed over me and I tried to process what was happening. For twenty years, whenever I had encountered a speed bump in my health, doctors had been able to right the ship again. I often had to be hospitalized for a few days, get some rest, or change a dosage of medication, but things always stabilized. For the first time in my life, a doctor was telling me that I was out of options.

I worked fiercely to hold back tears, while simultaneously trying to process the news. My doctor was telling me that I was dying. We had reached the end of what medical interventions could do...with the exception of one long-shot.

"Your only option now is a heart and double-lung transplant, but the chance of you getting one in time is very, very small," Dr. Howlett told me.

I can't say for sure that I even registered the last sentence he spoke. I heard something about transplant, but wasn't sure what that meant exactly. We'd spoken for years about the possibility that someday I may need a heart transplant. It had always been something that was going to *maybe* happen someday. And never had there been any mention that I may need new lungs too.

In the midst of complete overwhelm, something within me spoke out. I wanted to know the numbers. I wanted statistics, probabilities. How badly did I need this transplant? How long could I survive without one? What were the chances I would receive one in time? And if somehow organs were found, what were my chances of surviving the surgery?

I thought if I knew the numbers it would make me feel better. I was looking everywhere I could to find some sense of control in an uncontrollable situation, but medicine is not an exact science. Every patient, and every case, is different. There were so many variables in play in my case. There was really no way to know the outcome.

Dr. Howlett looked at me and responded the best way he could, "I'm not sure. If I had to guess, I would say that without a transplant, you might live another eighteen months, maybe two years."

Two years? Did he just say two years? I was twenty-three years old! How could it be that I only had two years left to live? I tried to wrap my mind around it, but I couldn't. Somehow, despite years of dealing with illness, always knowing that someday my heart would give out, it never seemed totally real. You never think the day will actually come, and when it does, all of the preparation time doesn't make it any easier.

I wasn't going down without a fight. I asked about the transplant. How could we do that? What was involved? What did I have to do? How soon could we get that done? Dr. Howlett explained that heart and double-lung transplants were rarely done. There were only three medical centers in the country where they performed the surgery, and before I could be put on the transplant waiting list, one of them would have to accept my case. There was little hope that anyone would be willing to take the risk.

What he shared was not exactly optimistic news, but I knew it was the only viable option. I wasn't going to go home and wait to die. And so, I asked Dr. Howlett if he would send my file to a Toronto hospital, to see if the team there would look at me as a possible transplant candidate. Reluctantly, he agreed.

It was nearly four months from that day before I was examined by the team in Toronto. They ran me through a battery of tests and eventually decided to roll the dice on me. I learned years later that there was a forty-five-minute debate among the medical team over my case. Many didn't think the risk made sense. The odds of survival were too small. Thankfully, someone in that room decided to take a chance on me.

We were told that once I moved to Toronto, I would be listed for the transplant.

In October 2001, my father and I left my mother and three brothers at home and moved to Toronto to wait for the transplant. We moved in with my Dad's cousin and started waiting for my pager to beep. The wait was grueling. Every day I lived on edge, hoping that today would be the day. Every day the pager didn't go off was one day closer to death.

After four months of waiting, it was decided that my health was too precarious to be an outpatient. I needed constant surveillance. I was admitted to hospital. Not knowing how long I'd be there, we tried to embrace the idea that this would be my new home for an indefinite period of time. I lived in that little room for nearly six months. Each day, I prayed for a miracle to save my life. Each day, I would go to sleep praying that I would wake up again in the morning.

On September 6, 2002, at 10:15p.m., my nurse appeared at my door, "There is a call for you at the nurses' station," she said. This was strange to me, because I had a phone beside the bed in my room. In six months, I'd never received a call at the nurses' station. I walked down the hall, picked up the phone, and heard a voice on the other end speak the words I'd prayed to hear for nearly a year: "Mr. Black, I think we have a set of heart and lungs for you."

The nurse on the phone gave me a few more details about what would happen next and when, if things went well, I might expect to go into surgery. I walked back to my room, somewhat in shock, and picked up the phone to call my Mom.

"Mom, I just got the call."

Mom traveled to the hospital, while I prepared. When she arrived, we hugged, cried and prayed. It would be hours before the surgeons would come to get me, and we knew that there was still a possibility that the organs would not be suitable for transplant and the surgery would be called off.

Thankfully, we were found out later the next day that the organs looked good and the surgery would go ahead. We prayed for the donor family who we knew were experiencing a much different moment than we were at that time. A few hours later, surgeons arrived and I was wheeled into surgery. "I'll see you soon" were the last words I spoke to my Mom.

I was in surgery for eight hours and in the intensive care unit for nearly a week, but I survived. In fact, my recovery went as smoothly as anyone could have hoped, and I was discharged sixteen days post-surgery. That was thirteen years ago. It's hard to believe. In some ways, it feels like a lifetime ago… and in another way, it feels like it was yesterday. There is no question that what happened has completely changed every aspect of my life. It has caused many challenges, but it has also given me much more than I could have ever imagined.

I'm now been blessed with the good health to be able to run marathons (four of them), and compete at Transplant Games in France, Canada, and South Africa. Most importantly, I was given the chance to be able to meet my wife, and bring three beautiful, healthy children into this world. Life truly is good.

It's ironic that I now write about the gift of this experience. We often refer to transplant as the gift of life, and there is no question that is true. In some ways, however, it was the illness that preceded the transplant that was the greater gift. The lessons learned in facing death have forever changed my life for the better.

Facing death at twenty-three was never part of my plan for my life, but then again, who can promise that life will follow our plan? As a speaker, I now ask my audiences to consider the possibility that life is actually supposed to be hard – that there is something inherently beneficial to being forced to struggle. Our character and humanity are shaped far more by the difficult times we experience than the easy ones. That said it is far too facile to paint my illness as nothing but a great blessing.

It sounds noble and inspiring when people say, "I wouldn't trade my experience for anything," but if we were really given the choice, what would we choose? If you could give back the biggest difficulty in your life, would you?

It's taken me a long time to get to the point where I have accepted the fact that it doesn't matter what I would choose, because I didn't get to choose. In fact, the whole idea that we have control over our lives is misleading. We control a lot of variables in our lives, and I'm a big believer in doing the best you can with every variable. However, we will never have control of everything. Illness, accidents and even relationships all have aspects that we have absolutely no control over.

The question isn't what would you do if you could do it again? The question is: are you willing to accept what you cannot change so that you can focus on what you can change? For better or worse, we are all dealt different cards in life. Whether you draw a full house, or you get stuck with a low pair, matters far less than how you play your hand.

There is no doubt that my experience with my health has taught me a lot. The journey has left me with many scars – both literal and figurative – but it has also given me great insights and blessings. There is one that stands apart from the rest, because it has had such a dramatic impact. That blessing is the gift of perspective.

When you talk to someone who has gone through a life-changing experience, one of the things they will likely talk about is how it has affected the way they perceive the world and their life. After facing death, somehow a traffic jam doesn't seem quite so problematic. I've learned that everything is relative, and that things could almost always be worse. Maintaining this perspective helps me to stay calm when others might get flustered. There are very few things that can get me upset. Compared with knowing I could die, most things just don't seem worth worrying about.

My transplant it not a cure; it is a treatment. The doctors have always been clear about that. The five-year survival rate of my transplant is fifty percent. I'm at year thirteen. The odds are good that I won't see my forty-fifth birthday. As a result, I'm probably more cognizant than most of the fragile and temporary nature of life. However, that's doesn't mean I live with reckless abandon. I wasn't supposed to make it to my twenty-fifth, thirtieth or thirty-fifth birthdays either, but I've lived to see all of them. I don't believe in the old adage that you should *live every day like it's your last*. Instead I just strive to be alive every day, and to enjoy and fully live each moment as best as I can. I do so because I know all too well, that one day it will end.

Perspective has also forced me to live a more prioritized life. It is one I encourage you to live as well. We all have priorities. I hope you've taken the time at some point to consider what your priorities are. The tragedy for most of us is that the way we live our lives does not reflect our priorities. If I asked you what your priorities are, what would you say? Most people who are asked that question will provide the same collection of predictable and logical answers: family, faith, friends and health. There are variances in the order, but for the most part, the answers are consistent.

In my work as a life strategy coach, I often ask others how closely their schedule matches their list of priorities. This is where it gets tough. If we're honest with ourselves, most of us, myself included, struggle to consistently live our lives according to our priorities. We say our family is the most important thing, but we work overtime and check work email at home instead of playing with our kids. We say health is important, but we go through the drive-thru and skip exercise because it's more convenient. We say our friends are important to us, but we never seem to find time to call any of them.

I've never had someone say that their number one priority was their career, though I've seen many people live as though it is. I've also been that person. I've never heard anyone say that sports, hobbies, or their smart phone were their number one priority, but I've seen people whose lives would say otherwise.

If I can share one lesson with you from my experience, it's this: work on living your priorities. The closer you get to having your schedule and your list of priorities align, the happier and more effective you will be.

Prioritization becomes a cinch when you have perspective. It's easy to decide what needs to be done and what doesn't when you properly understand what matters and what doesn't. Staying aligned with your core values is easier when you have perspective. That was my gift from a lifetime of heart-centered hits.

About Mark

BIO:

Mark Black is a heart and double-lung transplant recipient, turned four-time marathon runner, author, coach and speaker. Born with a life-threatening heart defect, Mark underwent two open-heart surgeries before the age of one. He battled his limiting condition for twenty-two years quite successfully, before being faced with the biggest challenge of his life. His heart was failing and without a rare and dangerous heart and double-lung transplant, he would not likely see his twenty-fifth birthday.

Since receiving his second chance at life, Mark hasn't wasted a moment. He has impacted the lives of more than 100,000 people through over 350 presentations across North America. His shares his truly unique story and powerful life lessons that help others live life with passion and purpose.

Mark lives in Moncton, New Brunswick, Canada where he spends as much time as possible with the most important people in his life: his wife Marise, and their children.

Website: www.markblack.ca

Mark Black

Patricia Arnoldin

HIT:

After a lifetime of sexual, physical and psychological trauma, Patricia was left a frightened young woman overwhelmed by facing life without knowing of the good within herself or the world around her.

GIFT:

By choosing to allow her abuse to spur a deep-rooted awakening, Patricia catapulted herself into a life of experiencing joyous love and recreating herself from the very core of her being.

Finding Myself
— *PATRICIA ARNOLDIN*

I'll never forget my third birthday party… and not because it was a really fun cowgirl party with all of my neighborhood friends. It was because my uncle was in the room, and I wished for him not to be there. At the time, I didn't comprehend what was happening behind closed doors, except that I didn't like it. Now much older and wiser, I know to call what happened to me sexualized violence. I can't tell you exactly when it started, except that it was before my third birthday, and that it lasted until I was nineteen years old.

On January 1ˢᵗ, 2001 a horrifying memory jolted the core of by being. The first of countless repressed memories came to my conscious awareness. Shattered, confused, and scared, I had only Andrew, my partner of six weeks, to turn to. At nineteen, I had moved to a new city, had only a few friends, and no family close by. Starting anew may have been what I needed to find comfort elsewhere. One thing I know for sure was that I needed to be safely away from the man who violently and sexually abused me for most of my life.

The next year was largely characterized by what my feminist therapist referred to as 'flooding,' or horrific and violent memories that overwhelm the unconscious and conscious mind. Therapy became a weekly event, sleep was minimal, and fear was so common that it felt natural. Anorexia, an illness I battled as a teen, found its way back into my life, as I desperately attempted to maintain any sort of control. Andrew would find me shaking in fear, hiding in strange places, and blaring music in an effort to drown out the sound of my uncle's voice in my head. I could, quite literally, no longer recognize my very own reflection in the mirror. I felt as though I was watching myself from the outside. The vivid flashbacks and disturbing truths continued to surface to the point where I had no other choice but to drop out of university.

In April of that same year, my grandfather fell ill and was soon to pass away. Going to see him meant having to see the man who wreaked such havoc on my life. I distinctly remember sitting in the hospital at my grandfather's side when fear took over my body. There was nothing I could do, and nowhere I could run. The only people who knew what had happened were Andrew and my therapist. I was terrified and I couldn't show it. In an attempt to protect myself, I went completely numb.

At the time, I thought my numbness was weakness. I now know that it was true strength. My intuitive body had taken ahold and enabled me to carry through a horrifying time without bringing me back to a place of victimization. Not long after my grandfather passed, the pain came flooding back, and I attempted suicide. Perhaps seeing *him* one more time had pushed me there, or maybe it was the devastating effects of memories and emotions. I was done.

Admitted to the psychiatric hospital, I was diagnosed with a dissociative disorder and Post Traumatic Stress Disorder (PTSD). Being labeled as a 'sexualized violence survivor' really bothered me. I felt unbearably ashamed and lost. I remember lying to the doctor, convincing him that I was okay. I knew that in order to get out of that dreadful place, I needed to tell the professional that I was happy to be alive and would never make such a foolish mistake again. When I got out of hospital, I realized the damage I had done by *outing* myself. People who I thought cared about me began to refer to me as 'damaged goods.' As numb as I was, the pain of their words hit hard. Suicide continued to occupy my thoughts when I sat in silence. Andrew and my mom remained close by, keeping a watchful eye on me.

Almost a year beforehand, my dad started seeing someone who was to become a guiding light in my healing journey, and my life. Dad and Jackie lived on the other side of the country, so I didn't see them often… but that didn't stop my relationship with Jackie from growing. As a fellow survivor, she understood me, offering support through email and telephone conversations. She sent me self-help videos and suggested I explore yoga and meditation. I purchased some Rodney Yee videotapes and gave yoga a try. It was just a form of exercise, right? I've always been pretty strong and flexible, so I knew I could do yoga.

Months later, as I continued with yoga, I began to feel restless during savasana (a restorative pose). As if driven by impulse, I would quickly rise upon completing the posture portion of the session and go for a 10km run! I told myself it was because I didn't *need* to rest in savasana (practiced at the end of class). Something about yoga scared me so much that I had the undeniable need to run as fast and as hard as I possibly could, daily. I was in great physical shape, but I was not well emotionally. I struggled to share my emotions, for fear of appearing weak or becoming a burden.

Yoga is a practice of releasing toxicity – be it physical, emotional, or spiritual. Not realizing what was happening, I felt triggered and went into flight mode, running away from what plagued me. I considered ending my relationship with yoga, but something kept me there. Intuitively, I knew that yoga was healing. It was awakening something within me that was terrifyingly unknown, yet oddly familiar. The more I practiced, the more I realized that what was rising from within me was just *me* – albeit, a part of me I had never met before.

It was scary for me to connect with myself, given that I was still being flooded with horrific memories. There were many postures that rendered me in tears. I felt terribly vulnerable… and yet, I kept finding my way back to yoga. The practice was affecting me in ways I could not fully comprehend.

For many years, I practiced in the comfort of my home. With the help of my therapist, I came to realize that the triggering poses were my releasing memories that I had embodied. I was getting stronger, little by little. Throughout those years, with my yoga mat under my feet and the support of my mom, dad, Jackie, and Andrew, I found my way back to university and completed my undergrad. In 2004, Andrew and I got married. I sincerely felt as though life was improving.

In the summer of 2006, I received the devastating news that Jackie had been diagnosed with ALS. I was terrified. I wasn't healed yet, and I didn't know how I would heal without her. I desperately began gathering every bit of wisdom from her brilliant mind, while supporting her with the belief that she would be the first to find a cure for the indomitable disease. With the fear of losing Jackie looming, I sought out a way to feel closer to her, even if it scared me. Several months after a new yoga studio opened down the road, I braved its doors.

Michelle, our instructor (and later my personal teacher), was powerful, confident, tender, enthusiastic, and truly cared. Every time I went to her class, she made me feel safe. It was likely due to the combination of her energy, words, touch, and a loving awareness that I was a person, rather than a victim of sexualized violence. Her ways enabled the depths of yoga to move within me.

One day in class Michelle asked us to dedicate our practice to someone in the world who needed it more than us. As I lay in savasana, energetically sending Jackie the healing benefits of my practice, tears streamed down my cheeks. In that moment, I pondered the effects of yoga moving to depths far beyond the surface, and the personal healing benefits of supporting and giving back to others. It was during these classes when I began to linger in meditation, experiencing moments of stillness. What was perhaps most magical about this time is that I began to notice a peacefulness after my yoga practice, especially if I was brave enough to release into savasana. This was the first time I was able to sit with the traumatic memories bubbling up in my body and recognize that it was a process of experiencing and releasing.

I became curious about the part of myself that was growing and coming to light. Was this my true Self? For the first time in my life, I began to experience something odd and uncomfortable: confidence. I began to dream a little bigger than ever before, soon applying to a Bachelor of Social Work (BSW) program. It was my vision to bring yoga to survivors of sexualized violence.

The program was both triggering and cathartic. I spent hours crying and longing for the comfort of my yoga mat. My professor, Dr. Carolyn

Campbell, gently encouraged me to experience the rising discomfort and allow it to foster internal growth. It wasn't easy, as I continued to struggle with showing emotion in public. I was so fearful of appearing weak or burdening to those I loved. Living in a sexist society that often blames women for their experiences of sexualized violence also left me feeling humiliated. This, alongside years of abuse, made it difficult for me to consider my emotions surrounding the sexualized violence. Acknowledging the label of 'survivor,' alongside the abundance of emotions that surfaced through the BSW program, brought my experience of dreadful shame to new heights.

It felt wrong to stifle my emotions. I had to find courage and give myself permission to experience copious amounts of feelings. Unsure of how to go about doing so, I called on Jackie's wisdom. She explained that our western world has created great disease because of emotions being pushed below surface level. She shared that a true warrior gives space for emotions, as they naturally ebb and flow throughout our lives. Jackie's words rang clear and beautiful: "To allow oneself to be vulnerable is a sign of strength."

Not a day goes by that I don't think of Jackie's words and the impact they've had on me, my healing journey, my yoga practice, and my relationships. It would have been easier to remain numb, though I knew that I had to make a frightening commitment to feeling some devastating truths that so often left me crumbled for days. The combination of Jackie's wisdom, Michelle's yoga instruction, and Carolyn's encouragement saw me through this very emotional time.

As I continued to work closely with Michelle, she helped bring up everything I had previously resisted during years of home practice. Michelle had a way of bringing life lessons and what I felt the off the mat yoga into the physical practice. I began moving to a place of experiencing what was happening within my body and mind. I needed to know more. After graduating from the BSW, I decided to begin my yoga teacher training.

Every experience and influential individual who came into my life during my healing – from feminist teachings and therapy, guidance from Jackie, Michelle's meaningful yoga, and an empowering teacher training – helped me realize that the abuse I suffered helped to shape who I am today, in a positive way. What happened brought me to the path of yoga and becoming a yoga teacher. It brought me to becoming a feminist therapist, and it immensely deepened my empathy. Most of all, it brought me back to my Self. This realization should have felt like a weight lifted from my shoulders, and yet, it began to enrage me. I spent quite some time feeling angry that I was a better person or a deeper person because of something so horrific. Many times I said, "I would rather be less empathic and have not been abused." It infuriated me when someone would cast light on the abuse by focusing on the wisdom or strength that I had gained. Yeah, I'm resilient. I had to be. But I didn't give a fuck about that. My entire childhood and youth were stolen from me. My innocence was drowned within the sea of my uncle's betrayal. I can't even say what my life was like before the hit of sexualized violence, because it doesn't exist.

The anger and resentment that had been left pent up for years inside of me had come to surface. The hatred was so putrid I could taste it, yet the thought of expressing it frightened me beyond comprehension. Working through these aggressive feelings was one of the most challenging phases thus far. I was triggered by memories of times I tried to retaliate during the abuse and was reprimanded. Society's deep-rooted views on how a woman should behave made the experience even more torturous. The fear arising from within me was debilitating at times; and yet, for reasons unknown, I persisted.

Little did I know, I was working through a very important phase of grief. I was grieving the loss of myself – the loss of nineteen years marked with sexualized violence. I was reclaiming my personal power as I began to comprehend that the shame I was experiencing was not mine. It was *his*. As I connected with this truth, I felt empowered. For the first time I decided that my title of survivor of sexualized violence was not a secret anymore. I couldn't hide anymore, and I no longer feared being judged by social stigma. I was finished questioning my self-worth, realizing that the shame I had felt belonged to my uncle, and it was misogyny that wrongfully forced it upon me fueled my fire. Though even after claiming my personal power, I remained angry. I realized that I needed to forgive him in order to completely release the pain and anger, and to truly explore my Self.

While I previously thought that feeling the anger was the most challenging part of my journey, forgiveness was truly indescribable. I resisted it, yet it continued to find its way into my mind. With help from therapy, yoga, and Jackie, I began to realize that forgiveness was not for him, but for me. When I could forgive him, then, and only then, could I truly release myself of the chains of the abuse. I went to yoga, I practiced, and I cried in the back corner of the studio. As terrifying as it was – because it felt as though I was giving him a free pass – I found my way through and found the strength to let go. Closing the door of forgiveness opened numerous bright and brilliant pathways before me.

Sadly, at this same time, Jackie lost her battle to ALS. As I reflected on her life, her strength, and her spirit, I knew I had to carry on with our dream. Jackie and I had so often spoken about creating a wellness center, where I could help others heal through yoga and feminist therapy. I knew that my greatest joy would be to pay it forward for all of those who had helped and guided me throughout my healing journey. Jackie taught me that if I knew some helpful piece of knowledge, it was my responsibility to share with those who need it…just as she had for me. With her wisdom in mind, I knew that I had to pursue my dream of bringing yoga to survivors of sexualized violence. I applied to the Master's of Social Work (MSW) program.

As I near the completion of my MSW degree, I am privileged to reconnect with the kind, deep, and meaningful Dr. Carolyn Campbell as I embark upon my master's thesis exploring how yoga can enhance the efficacy of feminist helping practices for women survivors of sexualized violence. As my journey continues to unfold, I am often reminded of all that I am and all that I have done over the past fifteen years, because of him. Because I am a survivor of sexualized violence, I was able to connect with myself in a way that may never have been possible. Every big decision I have made since my first repressed memory has been a direct result of the sexualized violence. Therefore, the path that I have chosen and am proud to be upon, is here because of him. For that I am grateful. I am grateful to him.

No longer do I have a need to hate him. The anger and hatred I held within was only ever toxic to me. After the years of abuse, and reliving the abuse through PTSD, I have found peace. I have gone through a myriad of emotions and have overcome countless hurdles. I don't want to hold on to negativity, especially something as heavy as hate. And so, I move beyond forgiveness and offer gratitude for my uncle's part in my journey. The release brought forth lightness and created a welcomed spaciousness in my mind and body. Clarity, if you will. This newfound openness empowered me even more. I had spent so much of my healing journey keeping my body physically fit so that I would be prepared to protect myself if I ever needed to again; however, I was also preparing and strengthening my mind. I now find myself physically strong and mindfully strong. Mindful strength is what propels kindness in the world.

Every survivor has a very different story. My goal is not to be a token for women survivors of sexualized violence. I can only confidently say that what happened to me was supposed to happen. I know this because I belong on this path. It is my dharma, or the path I was meant to follow. I feel it every morning as I wake. For years, I wondered why it all happened. Today, I can clearly see that the gifts I have received, and the gifts I continue to receive, are plentiful. Through the process of healing and forgiving the unforgiveable, I dug deeper within myself than I likely ever would have. By connecting to the depths of my Self, I was able to make meaningful connections within and with others.

I am inspired and live passionately. My passion, like all of the major decisions I've made, comes not only from the experience of trauma, but also from the experience of healing. It is this passion that has inspired me move from the counseled to the counselor, and the student to the teacher, whilst forever remaining as the counseled and the student so as to continue on a path of growth. The ability to linger within both simultaneous spaces has perhaps been one of the greatest gifts of this journey. It is this place of dualities that keeps me humble, keeps me growing, keeps me inspired, and keeps me caring for myself.

Through all of the therapy and yoga, anger and tears, I not only found my Self; I was able to forgive myself. After years of self-destructive behavior involving drugs, alcohol, physical abuse, anorexia and more, I realized how angry I was with myself and my body for allowing the sexualized violence to happen. It took quite some time for me to see that the manipulation and violence was such that I was not privileged with a choice in the matter. Now, for the first time in my entire life, I am able to say that I love my body and myself. As an adult, I have fallen in love with myself, and that is a beautiful gift.

I have children now. I refuse to let them grow up in a world where anyone should feel shame for pain that was unfairly inflicted upon them. Releasing myself of this shame moved me from survivor to thriver – a title I proudly claim. Throughout this journey, I was safely challenged to do the unthinkable: acknowledge that I was raped, I was molested, I was beaten, I was scared and scarred, and I was damaged. I was simultaneously challenged to realize that none of that was who I am. This stimulated the profound realization that I am a passionate, strong, confident, and empowered woman. Now, as I live my dharma, this is the energy permeates the air I breathe. With each day that I am able to move forward with this work, I find deeper healing – healing that has moved beyond my mind and body into my soul. The beauty of a passionate life is that we can move beyond finding ourselves into creating ourselves. And as we release what no longer serves us, we can uncover our passion and can truly begin living.

About Patricia

BIO:

Patricia is a Halifax-based yoga teacher currently working on her Masters of Social Work thesis, exploring how a yoga practice can enhance feminist therapy with survivors of sexualized violence. Tricia and her partner Andrew have been blessed with three children: Nathan and twins Mila & Laya. They are some of her biggest teachers, often found playing yoga beside her. Aside from being a mom and student, Tricia is most often found on her mat, practicing or teaching. She believes wholeheartedly that yoga is a first and foremost therapy, releasing the stress we place on our body every day from social pressure, past trauma, or day-to-day struggles. One of her goals is to be a part of the change in bringing yoga forward as a recognized form of embodied therapy for survivors of sexualized violence.

Website: www.yogawithtricia.com

Patricia Arnoldin with husband Andrew and children
Nathan, Mila, and Laya

Peter Davison

HIT:

As a free-minded bachelor, motivational speaker and adventure traveler with a healthy lifestyle, Peter was stunned and ashamed to get diagnosed with Parkinson's disease at age forty-five and spiraled into dark denial.

GIFT:

Parkinson's disease called Peter's bluff on a decades old belief that he was unworthy of love. After surrendering his heart, his world blossomed into a life unimagined as a first time dad and a future worth looking forward to.

The Queen of Hearts Called My Bluff

– PETER DAVISON

For about a week in May 2005, every time I stepped into the shower after my early morning run, my legs would shake like a leaf for several seconds. Other subtle symptoms became noticeable soon thereafter, and they persisted. As I would mindfully try to sign my name or brush my teeth, my right hand would not do what I wanted to. I thought to myself, "That's odd."

At my annual physical in July 2005, I mentioned my symptoms to my doctor, only to have him give me a puzzled look. It was as if he too was thinking, "That's odd." He referred me to a neurologist. By October, I was sitting in the neurologist's office performing a series of movement tests. As he watched me attentively, his eyes peering over his glasses, I completed exercises like tracking his finger with my eyes as he moved around my field of vision, scrunching up and relaxing my face, tapping my fingers on the opposite palm, flipping my flat hand back to front and back again, and a reflex test with a rubber hammer.

He took a long breath and said, "This is odd, but I think I know what this might be. You either have a brain tumor or Parkinson's disease."

I was gobsmacked, as though I had gotten hit square upside the head. Was there a door number three? Leaving the appointment, I sat in my car alone for what seemed an eternity, my thoughts locked in shock. I knew more than I cared to about my two options.

My dear Aunt Polly had been diagnosed with Parkinson's years prior. The throws of the disease left her body in constant movement, except when she was asleep. I had always admired how she radiated faith and grace, right up until the end of her life. As my tale unfolded, I was buoyed by her empathy and enduring love. My friend Luis had known the other option, and was grateful his doctor had caught a small tumor on his brain in the early, curable stages. Unfortunately, he died from a hemorrhage as they were performing a simple biopsy to determine if the growth was cancerous or innocent.

The next thought that came to mind, lingering and congealing over the many months to come, was that if my symptoms were so subtle, and only noticeable to me, how long could I get away with bluffing good health? Maybe my progress would be so imperceptibly slow that my parents, both in their seventies, would pass away before I'd have to put them through any worry. It was a stream of thought that began a slippery slope rationalizing denial, fueled with embarrassment and shame.

I was pissed off. What the hell was I doing with an *old person's disease*? I was only forty-five. I had been a vegetarian for a dozen years, never drank, smoked or did drugs, exercised regularly and used no harsh chemicals in my house. Just four years earlier, I had trekked ten days deep in to the Khumbu Valley of Nepal to the base camp of Mount Everest and summited Kala Pattar at 18269 feet. Even gasping for breath while attempting to oxygenate with fifty percent less air then at sea level, it had felt magnificent to be alive. I was in the best physical shape of my life.

An MRI ruled out a tumor, as a year of hosting my own private pity party rolled along. I wasn't dysfunctionally depressed, but I felt deflated. I was later told that my young niece had questioned why Uncle Pete didn't seem to be as funny. In my state, I even wrote a country and western the song to capture the mood: *I lost my dog, I lost my truck, I lost my health, I'm out of luck, just got PD, now what the f - - - ! Now my life don't look so pretty, on the road to pity city!*

The hit of being diagnosed with an incurable degenerative disease was more than just a health challenge, it also triggered my decades old belief that I was unworthy of love.

What seemed like a lifetime ago, in 1985, I had married my best friend. We had separated after only two years through painful, but mutual, agreement. Divorce challenges our self-worth, and surfaces what most social humans fear: rejection. I was no different. After we separated, I spent four years living in the dank cool basement apartment at my grandparents' home with their prayers holding me. The pity party had begun.

While there were glimmers of hope of finding love again, I was never able to totally trust and reveal all of my heart to a partner. I chose to focus my passion on my career, traveling as an international speaker. I saw a lot of sunsets in pretty cool countries, and I ventured solo more often than with a partner in my life. When I managed to date, I found myself in the cycle for only two years, or less. I may have been creating my own 'out' each time, always getting close, but not too close. I would also be critical, finding reasons to 'fix' my partners. Eventually, I would just stop participating and withdraw emotionally, until all hope of togetherness faded into amicable separation.

As my relationships became shorter, and I realized that I was playing my own personal game – one where I felt I couldn't lose, because I never played my full hand. I felt more like the joker than the king of hearts. There was no jackpot, as I put on my poker face and bluffed my way into and out of relationships. However, I hadn't fully given up being a romantic softy longing to love and be loved.

In April 2005, one month before my PD symptoms emerged, I was working Northern Ireland. There, my colleague and friend Tim Chapman invited me to his cottage in north coast village of Castlerock. The hill overlooking the village was a National Trust protected site, which featured a tumbled down castle and a striking intact rotunda called the Mussenden Temple, seated on the edge of the cliff overlooking the North Sea. As soon as Tim and I passed through the temple doors, I was struck by a deep presence of love and possibility. What I didn't know at the time was that the temple was built as a library by the fourth Earl of Bristol for his lover, Lady Mussenden, as a place where they could, 'read books' all day.

With the wind off the North Sea rattling the windows, I picked up a piece of broken floor tile and blurted to Tim, "I am going to put a marriage proposal under this floor tile and bring back the woman I love here to propose."

"That's great Pete," he affirmed, "but you don't have a girlfriend!"

"I'll work on it," I assured him.

That romantic intuitive flash of a dream to settle down with my true love and any hope contained within me vanished the next month when my symptoms first appeared and I started to literally shake loose my firm grip on my solo life. It felt as though Parkinson's was dealing the cards. The joke was on me. It was like the diagnosis was telling me, *so you think you are unworthy of being loved? Okay, I'll call your bluff and double down with an incurable disease gradually eroding your body and self-esteem, and then see how you hold your attitude.*

I entered a dark night of the soul, buying fully into my old attitude that I was unworthy of love. The spark went out within me, and it was all I could do was to continue to be a motivational speaker. As I delivered my talks, I began to grow uneasy that the message of my presentations was stirring up the uncomfortable challenge for me to walk my own talk.

The first realization of what was happening had begun the same day as my first neurology appointment, I had shared my signature speech message with nine-hundred high school youth. It was about recognizing and honoring the unsung heroes in our lives: those who support us through life's journey for a reason, a season, or a lifetime. I had begun the speech humming the classic tune "Lean on me" and closed by inviting another professional speaker, Will Njoku to join me in sharing about our unsung heroes growing up. Together, we broke into humming the familiar refrain of the song together and smoothly stepped back as members of the school glee choir continued the song and flowed onto the stage. It was a glorious celebration of support and belonging.

The irony that I wasn't honoring my own advice was not lost on me. The hypocrite within me had been found guilty. I kept out those who loved me and let my imagination drag me down, as I envisioned myself drooling, while sitting stiffly propped up in a wheelchair in a nursing home. I would be alone and that future was not friendly.

The Universe (or the working Spirit, God or the Grand Organized Designer), however, had other plans. In the late spring of 2006, I found myself lingering around after my regular yoga class and wound up staying for laughter yoga. The rules were simple: follow a series of physical activities that purposely create laughter, and fake it until you make it. The program was designed to open our body to produce endorphins – the body's happy juice. It also celebrates the maxim that laughter is the shortest distance between people. For the first time in a long time, I laughed and felt re-connected. I felt a lift of light and belonging.

What I learned through the class, I practiced myself and began to incorporate in my presentations. The most humbling of those sessions was with breast cancer and stage III prostate cancer survivors. The depth of the laughter from people who have looked death in the face and chosen to live fully was memorable and moving. It put my troubles, and my pity party, in perspective. After all, people typically die with, not from, Parkinson's.

Deciding to live my life more fully, I went to a music festival called Stanfest with my pal Oliver that summer. As I enjoyed the Friday evening performance from atop the hill, I glanced over to see a familiar face coming towards me. It was like a scene from the moors of the classic novel, *Wuthering Heights*. Andrea was dressed in light pink sailing jacket as she emerged out of the mist and into my arms with a big hug and a radiant smile. Eighteen years earlier, we had dated after meeting at a young adult's church group social club. That was back when I was still licking the wounds of rejection and projecting cynicism as a defense. As a self-righteous activist working for Greenpeace, I had criticized her for wearing leather and told her she had no fire in her soul. That was our last date.

This encounter was different. We were different. Andrea shared that she had recently separated, and I was open to receiving her presence. We joined our friends and enjoyed the music, danced and talked until the wee hours after the concert. Over the summer months, our attraction from all those years ago had rekindled … though I realized that if our relationship was to go any further, I would have to reveal to her what she was in for.

While camping one evening that summer, under the brightness of a full moon, with Van Morrison's "Moondance" playing in the background, I got up the nerve to share my diagnosis. I prepared myself for rejection. If my belief was that I was unworthy of love, this was to be the grandest test. All of my cards were on the table, my full house bet. The winner would take it all; the loser would fold and go home empty.

"I have a health condition that will affect the quality of my life as the years go on. You are important to me, and I want to share this with you," I told Andrea. "Last year I was diagnosed with Parkinson's disease."

She looked into my eyes, her face soft and golden like that of an angel and said, "So...now what?"

At that vulnerable risky moment, my heart opened and I teared up with a universal love that treats all things as being cherished and worthy. Excuses to hold back from living and loving from a place of low self-worth were indefensible. For the first time, I let the light shine fully shine into the dark and dusty corners of my murmuring heart and felt safe enough to surrender to something greater than myself. The gifts of my hit were beginning to unwrap, and my final surrender would be to let go and trust fall into the supportive arms of my family.

Andrea sat quietly holding my hand as I shared the news of my diagnosis with my entire family as they gathered for Thanksgiving dinner in October. They were sad, though also annoyed that I robbed them of the opportunity to offer a year's worth of extra caring and support. They told me they were there for me, always would have been, and always will be, because family love endures. I had crossed a positive threshold, and there was no turning back.

As Andrea and I grew closer in heart and commitment, we planned for a trip to Costa Rica together in January of 2007. Sadly, I still had hesitation about letting myself get too close in our relationship, and made an offhand comment about hoping she didn't think the trip meant anything. I hurt her before we even took the first step on our new adventure. It was a cruel and final the last gasp of the bachelor within me dying to his old ways of safe independent aloneness.

Our first eco-adventure was to climb Mount Chirripo, from which you could see the Atlantic and Pacific oceans on a clear day. The trail was brutal. It had fourteen markers, one for each kilometer along a worn path challenging us with an elevation gain of 6000 feet to base camp. It was a hard journey and we ached, ran out of water, lost our drive and purpose, faced fears, and encouraged each other to stop and smell the flowers and keep on going before we lost daylight. We made it to the lodge by sunset. The sun slipped below the ocean horizon, like an ascending orb that drops out of sight, leaving a final line of light that seemingly zipped up dusk. We had made the trek together and celebrated with rice and beans before the solar power cells in the lodge lost their charge.

We capped off the next day with our final assent to the summit. I was deeply moved by our success together. If we could make there, we could make it anywhere. In that sacred moment of possibilities, I felt my heart open once again. Inspiration filled me from how truly romantic a place the summit would be to propose. I also simultaneously recalled my dream to propose in Northern Ireland.

As the clouds rolled in below us, I shared honestly with Andrea: "This would be a great time and place to propose to you, but I'm not going to, because I have something else in mind."

Before she kicked me off the summit, I qualified it by saying, "Is it enough to say I want to spend my life with you and watch our last sunset together?"

For then, it was.

As we returned back down the mountain, to the city and internet access, the Universe intervened once again. In my inbox was an email invitation to speak at a national conference in Ireland that coming April. I replied yes and invited Andrea to come with me. She accepted.

When April arrived, we drove to our friend's cottage in Northern Ireland. It was two years to the day that I was moved to blurt out my romantic intention there at the temple. I had let Tim in on my plan, and he had placed a photo of Andrea and I at sunset in Costa Rica under the same floor tile, with a proposal written on back.

The next day, Andrea and I hiked up to the temple. While inside, she bent down and picked up a piece of floor tile to prop up the front of the camera so that we could take selfies. As fate would have it, she chose the very tile that had our picture under it. She made a puzzled comment as to how the picture got there, and then she noticed me kneeling, asking her what was on the back of the photo: "Will you be my partner for life? Will you watch the last sunset with me?"

Andrea said yes to life with me, and I said a hearty yes to living a full life with her. The gift of the hit of Parkinson's continued to unwrap. Once I surrendered to love, the Universe unfolded with gobsmacking abundance and blessings. It was almost as if it had been building up its plans for my life all along, but the world was waiting for me to get out of my own way.

Andrea and I were married on lucky July 7, 2007 at 7 o'clock in the evening. Thereafter, we rode the monthly roller coaster of hope and disappointment, trying for a baby. We endured a failed in vitro fertilization process, and fulfilled our nurturing need by bringing home a puppy to love.

In the fall of 2008, we received a call from my wife's twin sister Angela. She advised us to sit down. Bad news, I thought. It was quite the opposite. She asked us, "If a baby dropped into your lap, would you keep it?" Angela had secretly shared our profiles with an expectant sixteen-year-old, who was seeking suitable adoptive parents for her baby. We gleefully accepted, naming our little girl Hannah, or the 'gift of a child from God.'

Our story unfolded just as it had for some other childless couples who chose to adopt. Soon after Hannah came into our lives, we had Vance. He was born as a result of 'kicking it old school' in April 2011. Andrea was a statistical anomaly to get pregnant. She gave birth to a healthy boy two months short of her forty-sixth birthday. I was fifty-two, and a first time dad of two little kids. Somebody up there has a sense of humor!

It now seems lazy to dwell on annoying symptoms, like a complete loss of smell and taste, an unsteady voice and wobbly walking, because I have something much greater than a pitiful disease to wake up for. I cherish every moment with my kids, putting socks on, buttering toast, making lunches and walking to school. I am blessed to have so much beauty to look forward to in the foreground of my life, and I've learned how to keep my disease in the background, where it belongs. I am a full-time stay at home dad after retiring in 2014 when the symptom of my voice quality grew more *scrambly*, as Hannah would say.

While I don't know what the future will bring, I do know that I have a choice to step forward into the mystery alone or together. I also know that I needed a big kick in the arse to shake off my decades old belief that I was unworthy of love. I am grateful for the hit of Parkinson's and all the gifts that have unwrapped so far.

I shudder to think where I'd be today without the hit of Parkinson's. I give thanks for the pills that help me walk the kids back and forth to school and go on countless adventures building memories together. I am honored to have a partner for life with a soul that burns bright with passion for her career, and a dog-on-a-bone tenacity for what she wants… which includes me, as it turns out. Andrea had the courage to hold on for love, even though I tried to push her away. The universe had sent me the right partner, once I was ready for her.

I am now surrounded by love. The queen of hearts called my bluff.

About Peter

BIO:

The best thing that ever happened to Peter was getting diagnosed with Parkinson's Disease at age forty-five. He retired in 2014, after a twenty-eight-year career as a public school teacher, government family violence prevention trainer and international motivational speaker, because his voice was getting wonky. He now dedicates his passion and time as a dad to his daughter Hannah and son Vance. He is a Parkinson's educator and advocate, and a marketing advisor with Bedford Orthotics.

Peter founded Gift of the Hit Publications to fulfill his life-long goal to collect and share inspiring stories of people who have unwrapped blessings in their tragedy, adversity or setback to empower themselves and others to choose to live free of guilt and blame. His life's motto is: Go forth, do good, stay blessed and repeat as necessary.

Peter's autobiography, *Gift of the Hit*, much like his life, is a joyous work in progress.

Websites: www.giftofthehit.com
　　　　　www.peterdavison.ca

Peter Davison with wife Andrea Richard and children Hannah and Vance

Sheila Morrison

HIT:

When mental illness saw her eighteen-year-old daughter hospitalized and traumatized for fifteen years, Sheila fought an uphill battle for reform in mental health care to include compassion, respect and inclusion of the family.

GIFT:

Against professional advice, Sheila and her husband brought their daughter home, saw only possibility, nurtured every second of wellness, and in the process discovered within themselves a depth of compassion and love far deeper than they imagined possible.

Mother Bear Reflects on Loss and Recovery
– SHEILA MORRISON

The impact of a major earthquake or tsunami is fast and horrific. Sustaining a serious injury in an accident, or contracting a vicious infection, can be equally shocking and terrible. We offer compassionate care to those who suffer in such situations. On the other hand, some events seem relatively innocuous in the beginning, and grow more insidious over time, until one day you realize that the situation is beyond your control and compassionate care is not always forthcoming. In these cases, it is often only much later, looking back, that you realize the immensity of what you have been through.

Our daughter's brain seemed to begin to fall apart in her late teens. At eighteen, she began seeing a psychiatrist. At nineteen, she fell into a series of near constant psychiatric hospitalizations that lasted until she was thirty-four. She was robbed of her young adulthood of joyful curiosity and growth, and thus experienced a ruining of the potential for forming healthy adult relationships and a happy youth. Her decline from a sweet, funny, intelligent young woman thriving on books, acting, art and piano concerts, to someone with a severe unrelenting psychotic illness was devastating. Unresponsive to traditional treatments, we watched our child become disheveled, polarizing between being mute or screaming in terror, and responding violently to being touched, or to things and sounds invisible to us. Her eyes would roll up until nothing but the whites were visible – experiences that were both terrifying and without obvious cause. We looked to the expertise of our medical team to explain what was happening to her, in hopes of eventually finding a way to soothe this agonized soul and to bring our daughter back to us.

However, what actually happened was demoralizing and utterly painful. After our daughter was prescribed medications that made her symptoms worse, the hospital team determined that her case stemmed from a behavioral problem, and that we as parents were to blame for this shameful manipulative behavior. We should practice tough love, they said. They discharged her after a few months in the hospital. She was sicker than ever. That was our hit.

The illness was difficult enough in itself, but to pile on a callous disregard for who we were, for our integrity, and for our family history was truly trying. For two decades, we loved and celebrated our three accomplished and beautiful children, and there we were, faced with no sensible explanation for our daughter's dilemma. The only suggested course of action was to accept blame and kick her out of the family home. We, of course, did not.

With much trepidation, we found ourselves back in the emergency department before too long. For reasons of safety, we had no choice but to begin the process again. The barriers to progress remained the same, enhanced by the staff's disgust with our failure to understand their point of view. I became Mother Bear, as anger fueled my need to fight for my daughter's right to compassionate care. Communicating within the walls of the hospital seemed impossible, and so, I turned to the media to highlight some of the inadequacies of the mental health care system. The objective was not to point fingers at individuals, but rather to elaborate on the inadequate skill sets, crowded rooms, and understaffing that led to poor observational habits and corresponding volatile situations and patient injuries by untrained security staff. When the media captured the story, the powers that be at the hospital didn't deny anything. The response to my efforts was to transfer our daughter to another facility where we could start fresh. That was our sixth year in the hospital.

Starting fresh with a new hospital and staff, I went directly to top management (with my Mother Bear hat tucked behind my back) to discuss how I could be included as a member of the care team. It was clear to me that my daughter's illness had not previously been looked at in the context of the family, and that as a good parent, I had much to contribute in both evaluating my daughter's status relative to her normal state, and continuing to care for her on the days she was well enough to come home for a few hours. I wanted to be included in team meetings, and to contribute my own report of personal thoughts and observations. I also requested that I be able to make suggestions on therapeutic approaches other than medication.

Outside of hospital, I became involved in setting up the Mental Health Coalition of Nova Scotia – a group advocating for improving mental health care. I joined a group of physicians, as we explored the standards of care in psychiatric facilities. I sat on a committee of health professionals that would publish a book outlining resources and contact information for people who were experiencing a mental health crisis themselves, or in their family. I also spent a lot of time talking to other parents in positions similar to ours, along with young adults who had experienced a mental health crisis – individuals who were able to reflect on their experiences with illness and the care they received (or lack thereof) and support me. It was a time of great learning and accomplishment that made me feel I was contributing, if not directly to my daughter's wellbeing, at least to the state of mental health care in the province. Getting involved was possible only because my daughter was an involuntary inpatient, leaving me with time for the cause.

Back in hospital, a physician new to our case was puzzled by our story. She asked us if our daughter had ever been seen by anyone from genetics. She had not. What ensued was a diagnosis of Micro-deletion 22q11.2, popularly referred to as 22q. Our daughter was twenty-five years old and had been extremely sick for seven years.

Micro-deletion 22q11.2 is a syndrome that is second to Down's Syndrome in incidence. Despite its frequent occurrence, it is relatively unknown to physicians. Someone with the syndrome is missing a tiny piece of genetic material on a section (known as 11.2) of the long arm (called q) of the twenty-second chromosome. Those born with this syndrome can have any combination of 180 characteristics or deformities, depending on how large the deletion is, and where it is located. Many of these children have serious heart defects and require surgery in infancy or later. Some have problems with their palate, thyroid gland, skeletal or other structures. Others have various degrees of intellectual disability. Many require years, or a lifetime, of treatments, surgeries, and therapies. More often than not, their parents have a desperate time trying to find medical personnel who can look at the whole person, and the whole family, to help co-ordinate care.

Twenty-five percent of those born with 22q eventually develop various psychiatric issues, either in childhood or in their late teens. For some unknown reason, those who develop a psychosis, with disordered thinking and hallucinations, do not generally respond well to the typical courses of anti-psychotic medications. Our daughter (for whom the main feature of the syndrome was late onset mental illness) was seen by fifteen psychiatrists and had trials of countless medications with unbearable side effects and no relief, for thirteen years.

In November of 2008, our daughter was stable enough to be discharged from hospital. Her progress had been helped enormously by The Center for Addictions and Mental Health (CAMH) in Toronto, where psychiatrist Dr. Anne Bassett – internationally-renowned for her research and care for people with 22q – works in what is now called The Daiglish Family 22q Clinic (http:/22q.ca). After identifying that our daughter had the deletion, Dr. Bassett came to visit our family in Halifax and saw us in Toronto many times She consulted with all our caregivers.

While my ongoing involvement in the care team made things easier, there remained hurdles. On the day the hospital staff planned our daughter's discharge, they recommended she be placed in a locked facility. Such a suggestion seemed counterproductive and ridiculous. We took her home.

The next seven years proved to be a huge indicator of how important the psychosocial environment can be. Although her medication regime was no panacea, it proved sufficient to allow our daughter's brain to heal and new neural pathways to establish themselves. In 2008, she was unable to look around and take in her environment, make eye contact, speak with a stranger, or understand and follow instruction in a cookbook. Today, our daughter has wonderful observational skills and documents things with her camera that I wouldn't even notice. She can hold a pleasant conversation and take interest in others. Her computer skills have surpassed my own, and she writes, plays piano, trains her dog, makes art, and thrives on hiking in the woods. Ultimately, she was able to develop a small, successful catering business. In the first few weeks, the only task she could do was put frosting on cupcakes, and just barely. There were many, many steps involved in learning to work in a kitchen, which proved to be a wonderful place to work on organization, reading, math, hygiene, social relationships and many other things. She loves to bake and worked her way up to catering to weddings and house parties, as well as donating her baking abilities and creations to non-profit groups.

I have come to a place of peace. My Mother Bear hat is dusty. It is not lost, but reassuringly buried in a closet. We live a fragile wellness. Sometimes it fractures, but it more easily and quickly mends than ever before. This is time for reflection for me, and one to plan ahead for a time when I no longer need to play caregiver.

I am thankful for so many experiences I had before my hit – things that made me who I am, so I was equipped to deal with the medical system in a way that impacted on our daughter's care. At age twenty (the age at which my daughter was just entering the mental health care system), I left Canada with my new husband and spent seven years teaching school in remote villages in West Africa. We filtered our drinking water three times before boiling it. We learned the local languages and bargained our way through noisy outdoor markets for spicy peppers and vegetables, caught and carried live chickens home for dinner in a basket on a motorcycle, and cooked outdoors on a tiny charcoal grill made from a coffee can. We shared our spicy stews with the night watchmen in exchange for language practice. And when the cholera epidemic swept through West Africa, we volunteered in makeshift hospitals where patients lay elbow to elbow on concrete floors receiving intravenous fluids. That was when I learned how precarious life can be.

With no electricity, television, telephone and very little water, every moment in Africa was filled with purpose. We learned patience by discovering that with the right attitude, there could be joy in waiting an hour for a postage stamp. There, it was essential to inquire after the health of everyone's relatives before making a small transaction. Perhaps the greatest lesson gained through our experience was that my husband and I discovered we were a true team, giving and taking where it mattered most. We knew that hardships were easier because they were shared – an awareness that proved invaluable years later with our daughter. Such a gift became an essential part of our lives when things got tough.

After our time in Africa, I returned to university in Nova Scotia and became a physiotherapist. I quickly slipped off the traditional paths and became interested in people who lived with chronic pain. The experience also helped me gain some idea of how the hospital system worked. I knew what doctor and nursing notes looked like, how to write a physiotherapy progress report and a letter to a doctor, how to interpret some tests, and what questions to ask. What I didn't know was how mental illness is evaluated and treated, and what tough working conditions these staff faced. Nor was I aware of the severe degree to which stigma played a role in how staff viewed patients and their families.

My education and experiences taught me an important lesson that served me well in working with my daughter: that everyone has a starting point and needs to be able to see progress and feel rewarded for their efforts. That is what builds hope and healing. It sounds simplistic, but it is a principle rarely put into practice in either physical or psychiatric medicine, where clinicians can be stymied by patients with serious chronic illness. Interestingly, I discovered that my own colleagues who were frustrated by patients with chronic pain having a seeming inability to move forward tended to blame the patient for being irresponsible. *They have to want to get better* was the common refrain which I found shocking and unacceptable. The attitude of my daughter's first care team was similar.

What level of independence will my daughter now be able to attain? It is impossible to predict, and therefore hard to plan for the future. Paranoia keeps her socially isolated. Disturbing memories from her hospital years of being labeled, man-handled, fractured, locked up, and deprived drive her nightmares and cause her to lose deep sleep, leaving her tired and sad.

Cognitive impairments from illness, electroconvulsive therapy or medications make some tasks onerous, despite the huge gains she has made. There is always some hope that a new medication will come along that will help with her paranoia, PTSD, and cognition. It is not something I count on, however, given her poor response to medication over the years. Therefore, I look for alternatives such as training her dog to be a psychiatric service dog.

When my daughter's wellbeing required that I spend more time with her in her teens, I had gone back to teaching part-time at a school called SpellRead, which excels in teaching children and adults who find reading and writing difficult because they have not responded to the usual remedial programs. The fundamental principles of that role were about breaking a problem into its smallest units, ensuring success at every lesson, and rewarding every positive move no matter how small (with no negative feedback). These principles, which also underlay my approach with people living with chronic pain, became the basis for working with my daughter after she experienced so much trauma and negativity in hospital.

Change in mental health care is happening slowly. We have better awareness programs in schools (although access to community care remains lacking), more sensitivity training for first responders, and the beginnings of better programming for families. Still, services are pitifully inadequate and underfunded, and stigma still rears its ugly head. What happens to the adult children when parents are no longer around? That is the scary part. That is what keeps me focused on helping my daughter become as independent as possible.

I was never one to think about working one job until age sixty-five, and then having a retirement plan. Life, for me, isn't a straight line, but rather a series of points where the trajectory can change at any minute. Being open to possibility and change has been exciting, but surprises happen and I never anticipated that I would be a caregiver until the end of my days. No longer am I a paid health professional, though I work more hours in a day than ever before. I continue to assess, treat, re-assess, report, discuss, make notes, attend conferences, read, write, change care plans and counsel, as a mom and wife.

Our daughter now lives in her own apartment in our house. For a number of reasons, the alternatives to having our daughter be anywhere but home simply aren't feasible. We tried two government-provided care homes, though they never worked for our daughter. When the time comes that I can no longer be her primary caregiver, one possibility will be to hire someone to come into our home. Meanwhile, my challenge is to find ways to create new pathways for myself in order to keep my brain engaged and exercised. As our daughter gradually gets healthier, I incorporate joyful experiences into my own life in small snatches of time. They are always things that can be easily rescheduled when necessary. I take time for coffee with a friend, singing lessons, writing short stories, small art projects, training the dog, an outing with my husband, a visit to the gym, or a little volunteer work. Such activities fill in the tiny bits of time between caring activities. Slowly but surely, those slots of time are growing bigger and more frequent as my daughter learns to do things on her own. Every day brings something new for both of us.

Because of this experience we've shared together, I am much less extro-verted than I used to be. My circle of friends is also much smaller and includes only those who truly understand when I have to cancel a date at the last minute. For the most part, my true friends are people who have either experienced a mental health crisis or are close to someone who has. I have let connections go and have lost some conversational skills in certain scenarios, and I often choose to disregard chance opportuni-ties to re-connect in order to keep my own stress level low. I see this as a positive, having the wisdom to choose what is healthy for me. These changes to a quieter, more introverted life may be because I have had to tone down my exuberant nature in order to connect better with someone who is ill, or it may simply be because I have not had the time to explore the way I once used to as an actress and world traveler. Sometimes I miss the adrenalin rush of that life, but I am equally happy to sit on a rock and enjoy a sunset. My daughter has given me the gift of knowing how to sit quietly for a long time, breathe deeply and slowly, and be with what-ever is. Sometimes, those simple things in the moment were all I had to offer....and they helped.

There are other gifts as well. My two other children have become sensitive loving souls who know how to approach someone in pain. They have touched people. Through this journey, I have been able to support others who are living with someone going through a crisis, or be with people going through their own breakdown. Even my daughter recognizes other people's pain and frequently gives food, money and comforting words to the homeless, encouraging me to do the same.

Continuing care that offers a good quality of life in the community is almost non-existent and unlikely to happen in my lifetime. My dream is that my husband and I will live into old age and that our daughter will gradually need us less and less, as her circle of support widens. I envision a nanny or housekeeper who will be like family to us, helping to care for our daughter and for us. When we are gone, that new caregiver will be there to sit quietly and wait for the storm to abate. For this all to happen, I may need to win a lottery ticket, or perhaps it will all simply work out.

Although it is important to plan for the future some things cannot be predetermined. Most of the time, the present moment is the best place to focus our energy and grow just a little bit more. Looking back over the last seven years, I can see we have come a long way. Then again, I never doubted that we would.

About Sheila

BIO:

Never one to say no to an adventure, Sheila Morrison has traveled the globe and tried her hand at many roles – educator, physiotherapist, salesperson, actress, writer, public speaker, volunteer, dog trainer and closet singer. But the most rewarding job of all has been coaching her daughter to jump back into life after a serious long term illness related to a syndrome known as Micro-deletion 22q11.2.

Sheila speaks and writes extensively about mental health issues. She has contributed to www.ourhealthyminds.com, Women Who Care (Pottersfield Press 2010), www.understoreymagazine.ca, and The Globe and Mail Facts and Arguments. Sheila and her husband Jim Morrison live in Halifax, Nova Scotia, with their adult daughter and her service dog, a big cuddly chocolate poodle called Jade.

Sheila Morrison and her daughter

Joscelyn Duffy

HIT:

The winds of change hit fast and furious as Joscelyn's vast world of social and career possibilities narrowed to the confines of her home, as she spent her late twenties working through a debilitating and life-threatening case of lupus nephritis.

GIFT:

Fusing her knowingness gained in using illness as a healing guide with her abilities as a gifted writer, Joscelyn now helps others claim their personal power by trusting their truths, finding their authentic voice and living out their purpose.

Flying From the Cocoon
– *JOSCELYN DUFFY*

On the May long weekend of my twenty-seventh year, with one passing glance in a full length mirror, my life forever changed. My ankles, it seemed, had all but fully disappeared. They had been replaced with two elephant-like stumps, padded by nearly fifteen painful pounds of fluid. It had taken the mirror to reveal the truth of the physical imbalance that had been building within me.

The baffling disparity in my physical make-up stopped me in my tracks with its impressive stature. Because of the severity of my symptoms, doctors quickly unveiled the shocking root cause of my physical ailments: an advanced and life-threatening case of lupus nephritis (lupus that causes severe inflammation and protein loss in the kidneys).

While I had previously prided myself on nurturing my mind, body and spirit with healthy food, exercise and time for personal growth, my daily focus had been primarily about *doing* and experiencing all that life had to offer. I had been living a life whereby I scurried through my days, attempting to be a part of every social gathering, bask in physical activity outdoors, learn as much as possible from life, and embrace every challenge that came my way. Perhaps I was facing the epitome of what I always welcomed in my life: a good challenge and an incredible opportunity for learning and growth.

A whirlwind breeze had blown in to my life and rocked my world. There I was, soon nearly physically halted by legs rendered nearly immobile. My friends and family were in disbelief. I was perhaps still in shock, though attempting to rise to the challenge, as my stoic side would always do. It was humbling, however, when I had no physical choice but to surrender the life I had come to know and enjoy. In the seeming blink of an eye, gone were my social gatherings and athletic pursuits. My financial career was put on hold and relationships were challenged by the strain of debilitating illness. The shock of the situation left me perplexed, asking *why* such a shift had come my way.

Others wondered how a young woman who was so dedicated to healthy practices and spiritual awareness could be handed a life-threatening illness. I could have pondered the very same question at length's end, but I saw no value in asking *why me?* After all, I knew that a part of me had known that something had been *off* with my physical body…and perhaps even with the life that I *thought* I loved. Though putting allopathic medications into my system was difficult (given I had always preferred a natural route), the hardest pill to swallow was my own ignorance to a long-time calling from within.

Before my life was brought to a standstill with the diagnosis of lupus nephritis, my days were maximized between my challenging sales and marketing career, marathon training, social networking, team sports and time with friends and family. I had plenty on the go…though I had enough awareness to know that my mind, body and spirit had not always been happily heading in the same direction. Perhaps the world was (not so gently) directing me on a new course in life – one that would begin with a shake up like no other I had known.

The Cocoon

It's amazing how fast our reality can change. In what seemed like the blink of an eye, my world of exploration and enjoyment shrunk from vast lands of opportunity to the confines of the four walls of my home. I quickly came to understand just how a caterpillar might feel once it became fully grown and entered in to its cocoon stage.

Within a matter of weeks, I was thrown in to the fire of a laundry list of physical symptoms related to my illness and ill-effects of intense drug therapy. My body had become overwhelmed by what initially felt like a force grander than me. Mentally, I researched, processed and did my best to try and understand just what was occurring within my body. Emotionally, I had not yet even begun to comprehend the whirlwind diagnosis…though I at least had the stubborn determination to know that I would make it through whatever was coming my way. And I had not even *begun* to tap in to the spiritual revelations of my fate.

I wonder how gently the caterpillar's transition in to the cocoon occurs? Personally, mine felt like one of brute force, beginning with a rare complication of a massive blood clot in the renal vein of my right kidney (renal vein thrombosis) just several weeks in to my diagnosis...and the day of my twenty-seventh birthday.

Having already frequented the hospital for a kidney biopsy and a resulting hematoma, I made my way back to the emergency room of the hospital with a pain unlike any I had previously encountered. After seven hours of waiting (with my survival clearly in jeopardy), I was admitted into hospital with my family members by my side, and promptly pumped full of blood thinners to ensure that the clot diffused and didn't move to my lungs or brain and take my life.

After eight days in hospital, under constant monitoring, I was cleared from further threat and sent home...in the form of a walking science experiment. The blood thinners began to consistently throw off the course of my doctor-prescribed drug therapy treatments in every possible way. My condition was overwhelming at best, and a far cry from my previous practices of only ever choosing to use simple natural remedies. Given that my medical doctors had so bluntly told me that the alternative to following their prescribed course of drug therapy was an almost certain loss of my kidneys, and perhaps death, I obliged. It was a situation so harsh, and most definitely unlike any I had ever faced before. While there were moments of not knowing whether drug therapy felt right, I opted to trust my doctors.

When I walked out of hospital, I started anew in many ways. My physical energy may have been diminished and my body incredibly overwhelmed, but I felt more alive than ever before. I had stepped into a second chance at life. As I would look up at the bright blue sky on a summer's day, the clouds had never looked so fluffy and white, and the sun was never so warm on my soul.

Growing Legs

After the effects of the kidney biopsy, the blood clot and a week in hospital, I found myself unable to walk for more than a minute or two unassisted. It was a humbling time, given that just a few months prior, my legs had so easily coasted through ten to fifteen mile runs as a part of my marathon training. I also quickly learned that my recovery and return to life would not come without the assistance of others. It was time to shed some in my stoic independence and allow it to be replaced with a gracious interdependence. There were countless activities of daily living that had become nearly impossible feats given my physical limitations and the debilitating fatigue that had began to sweep over my body. The emotional support of those close to me became more critical than ever before, especially given that I faced a physical reality that left me wondering if I would be waking up alive each morning.

My life had become more mentally, emotionally and spiritually challenging than ever before. I had to adjust from no longer being a part of the financial community to my newfound job of bodily awareness. Forget tracking stocks in the market; I had a new ticker to follow. Through the sometimes overwhelming nature of the challenge before me, my stubborn determination and optimism continued to rule. Things were most definitely different, though I continued to have hope, because I knew that the strength and truths within me remained. I didn't know just how long it would take or how I would get there, but I did, without a doubt, know that I would return to the life I knew and loved.

For another year, my prescribed treatments carried on, without much significant improvement in my condition. I became like a caterpillar in a cocoon...with the bonus of a phone connection to the outside world. Much like the caterpillar, I suffered the heartbreaking loss of almost half my hair. To add fuel to the fire, the toxicity of the drugs led my liver to become dysfunctional, twice. When it became obvious that the drug therapies were simply not working for me, I knew that there had to be a better way – one that would be more gracious in the healing of my body.

Long days spent with no option but to rest in bed allowed me incredible introspective contemplation time and a new-found awareness of my physical, emotional and spiritual body. The most beneficial days in my recovery were those when I allowed hope and powerful positive thoughts to prevail. The power of my mind and spirit, along with the benefits of healthy nourishment and exercise had kept me feeling so alive throughout my life, and I knew they would also help me progress through that which sometimes felt like a potentially impassable illness. I believed in following a more natural treatment course with every ounce of my being, and chose to make it my sole (soul) focus…to the dismay of my medical doctors.

Growing Wings

Venturing into unknown territory was scary, especially when it involved my health and ability to live beyond such a trying condition. I walked into my doctors' offices and shifted the course of my treatment from unknowingly accepting medical prescriptions for an illness that I initially felt to be bigger than me, to taking ownership of my own health. While I had always been rather independent and stubborn, I had often used my knowledge and wisdom to comply with the standards of what was deemed as acceptable. Standing fully grounded in the holistic methods that I wholeheartedly believed in, I, for the first time, felt empowered with the sense of becoming a non-conforming free-thinker and master of my own destiny. My choice wasn't met with encouraging support by everyone, but it felt right for me, so I persevered.

My medical doctors called me crazy and even candidly told me that I had a death wish by thinking that I could heal myself with anything other than the potent prescriptions. At first their words were hard to hear, but over time I learned to stand my ground and simply agreed to disagree with what was, at the end of the day, simply a difference of perspective. For the first time in my life, I had come to be truly compassionate with myself and to live in full support of what I trusted to be true. It was a decision that bolstered my confidence and the joint efforts my naturo-pathic doctors and I plotted on the natural course to my healing.

Through my healing journey, I learned that perception has immense power. Every day, while healing in bed for hours on end, I would visualize myself being better and doing everything that I wanted to do. I would also go within myself to understand who I truly was, and what messages the illness may be attempting to reveal to me. My stubborn logic reassured me that there was no point in being upset or surrendering to the illness, because I had so much to look forward to once my visualization of good health transferred in to reality.

I also learned to laugh more. As countless bizarre symptoms plagued my body, I chose to laugh through the tears of physical pain and strain. When a year of dizziness became so intense that I could hardly walk straight, I joked about padding the walls of my home. When my short term memory was all but shot, I learned to truly laugh at myself and become totally at ease with making mistakes. And when extreme fatigue did not relent over two years, I simply did what I knew my body needed to do – I rested, with a smile on my face and peace in my heart. That was when I began to grow in awareness of what could be created within the mind while seemingly trapped in a bed dealing with a debilitating illness for more than three quarters of each day, for several years. As crazy as my life had become, perhaps it was all just as it was intended to be.

Every day in my healing journey meant a fresh start, and was one day closer to my full recovery. While it took time and patience, the healthy mantras that I repeated on end began to materialize in my physical being. Everything was a balance, between honoring my body's healing needs and pushing myself just enough to see progress. As my strength slowly began to return, allowing me a few decent waking hours in the day, I would push with every bit of my mental strength to get my body in motion via some form of exercise. Some days I sat on the training bike at the gym and hoped that I didn't have a dizzy spell and fall off. Other days, I stumbled outside in the fresh air and slugged my tree-stump-like legs through a walk until I found some minute sense of grace and fluidity. No matter how difficult it was to get physically moving, every dose of exercise helped me become that much stronger. There was never a day where I felt worse for having put my body in motion.

When more than one year of dizziness finally subsided, I chose to exercise my mind as well, by reading countless books to help my healing progress, and to build a greater understanding of myself, others and of life. My passion for creating also inspired me to keep moving forward, and had its own healing properties. A paint brush and canvases, or a pen and paper, became my creative outlets, whereby in a state of semi-waking consciousness, I would paint or write out my raw emotions and hopeful visions.

There was rarely a time that was easy as I continued to persevere; however, I chose to always allow positive intentions to prevail. When unfavourable test results led to my feeling as though I had taken one step forward and two steps back in my progress, I tried to take those little hits in stride and trust in all the hard work that I was putting in. My focus remained on fueling myself through my passions of creativity and exercise, and on continuing to believe that a full recovery was most assuredly in my near future. The stubborn determination that I had always held within turned out to be one of the greatest gifts in my healing.

The Butterfly

While in the cocoon, the caterpillar uses only what it has within itself to become a butterfly. As my time progressed, healing alone at home, I, the *loopy caterpillar*, began digging deeper within myself to grow to fly freely once again. While my world had shrunk to a much small geographic span, it had also expanded in many other ways. By having no choice other than to lie in stillness and recover for much of the time, I began to discover the exponential power to create and manifest what existed within me. I gained a true awareness of my own personal potential, and of the synchronicities of the world. Everything in life started to hold more value and to make more sense. Through the sometimes foggy moments of my physical ailments, there was the development of a heightened sense of clarity…on a wholly new level. Even the fact that I had been removed from the life I knew and forced to face a lengthy life-threatening illness at a tender age began to have meaning and purpose.

I learned to accept my situation (without surrendering to the illness), and was open to discovering the gifts that lay within it. I danced in a beautiful balance between the empowering feeling of controlling what I could (such as diet, rest, exercise and my thoughts), and the liberating sense of letting the ways of the world and actions of others play out as they may. I developed what I termed *active patience* – whereby I was patient with my body healing at its own pace, while actively putting in all efforts to help it along on the journey. Above all, I became in tune with my soul to an extent that I hadn't previously realized possible, and I gained a true appreciation for the simplicities of life. Through my experience with lupus nephritis, I learned that I could either question what life has thrown at me, or I could ask what there was to be learned from it. At some point in my journey, I came to fully embrace being a student of life, in all its astonishing surprises and challenges.

When the caterpillar is transforming into a butterfly within the cocoon it looks, from the outside, as if nothing is going on; however, we know that big changes are happening inside. My time spent in a *lupus cocoon* was not much different. In stillness and quiet, I experienced personal awareness and growth grander than ever imagined possible. As I regained even greater strength and opened my new wings to soar through life, it quickly became evident that the way in which I related to others had changed. Children began to see in me a child-like spirit, and I saw theirs. I was able to compassionately relate to the symptoms and sentiments of ailments of the young and old. And wherever I went, I forever felt a sense of being connected to a bigger, more synchronistic world. It was a world that I had discovered from within my healing cocoon, and was allowed the opportunity to explore with my once again fluidly moving legs … and wings!

Some call the cocoon stage a *protected stage of development*. I am now able to see that having to work through and overcome several years of the intensity of lupus was not the world removing me from all the activities that I loved, but rather the world resituating me in a place where I would undergo the growth that I was meant to in this lifetime. For many months of my illness, I simply longed to get better and return to the life and financial career that I had known. However, as time progressed and I began to dig within myself, I could see that I had in fact not be derailed, but rather set on a new course in life...one in which I would share with the world my story of personal power and our ability to compassionately heal. The hit of lupus was in fact a gift – removing me from a life where I *thought* I was happy, and unveiling with clarity a life where I *knew* I would be forever true to who I really was. All of my previous passions and abilities in the areas of speaking, writing and creativity had become fused with the powerful messages of the strength of the human spirit and honoring our personal truths. The intersections of the world I once knew pre-illness and the revelations encapsulated in my healing had shaped my new-found gifts to share with the world.

Metamorphosis is the process by which a caterpillar turns into a butterfly. It is perhaps one of the most highly depicted transformations of form and character. I myself had morphed from a young woman eagerly capturing life's opportunities, to a woman of studied wisdom and a depth of personal awareness, who was prepared to joyfully embrace and compassionately share every aspect of life. Through my creativity, writing and passion for words, I moved forth lending my compassionate heart to helping others find clarity of self, purpose and their ability to heal. There was an effortlessness to my new mission in life, perhaps because I had learned to simply *be* and trust in the journey that is life.

Through your life hits and the revelation of the gifts therein, I wish the same for you: a deep-rooted trust in life, a compassionate heart and the realization of your incredible personal strength.

About Joscelyn

BIO:

Creative Consultant, Ghostwriter, Author, Reiki Master and Motivational Speaker, Joscelyn Duffy offers a unique blend of compassionate wisdom, intuitively-inspired creativity and rich expertise in the contextualization of consciousness. She has fused the strength of her business background with years of personal introspection and healing to offer a unique intuitive approach to writing. With over ten books having streamed from the tips of her fingers and depths of her soul thus far, there is an unbridled passion within her for being the strategic storyteller behind pieces that move the masses. Her greatest passion is in helping others embrace their personal power, and the message echoing through her work is that of finding and fearlessly expressing the authenticity of who we are. Spend time with Joscelyn and you will be forever inspired to *Trust Your Truth, Find Your Voice* and *Live Your Purpose*.

Website: www.joscelynduffy.com

Joscelyn Duffy

Jeanie Cockell

HIT:

At the peak of her consulting career, resurging after breast cancer, continuing to live with an ongoing blood disorder, Jeanie woke up in a hospital bed with a crushed femur, broken pelvis and ribs, massive internal bleeding, concussion, punctured lung as a result of a car accident.

GIFT:

Being authentically ALIVE (Appreciate, Love, Inquire, Venture, Evolve) is a huge gift that Jeanie lives by and shares with others through writing, speaking, facilitating, teaching, coaching and consulting.

Being Authentically Alive
– JEANIE COCKELL

One day, I woke up in a hospital bed with a crushed femur, broken pelvis and ribs, serious internal bleeding, a concussion, and a punctured lung. I still have no memory of the accident that landed me in that bed. I do have a vivid memory of waking up feeling happy that I was alive.

The accident had happened when I was driving home from a successful two-day facilitation session. I was feeling very elated, and looking forward to seeing my partner, Joan. This time of our lives was full with interesting work and travel. We'd recently been to the Grand Caymans for a snorkeling holiday. Joan was just back from speaking engagements in the U.S. and Canada, and meeting with our future publisher. A couple of months prior, we'd spent a weekend celebrating my birthday in New York City. I was so pleased to have fully recovered my energy after a journey with breast cancer, and to be at the peak of my consulting practice travelling all over the world to facilitate, speak and consult. I had been to Bermuda, Qatar and Nepal, as well as multiple locations in the U.S. and Canada.

It had been a year since I had completed radiation treatments – the final phase of treating breast cancer. The radiation had been preceded by three surgeries over a three-month period. The surgeries had each been complicated by the fact that I take warfarin – a blood thinner – due to a blood disorder that in the past had caused blood clots in my lungs. I had lived and will live with this blood disorder until I die of something else. It will not kill me … though the side effects (e.g. blood clots) might. Daily, I take pills to keep my blood cells within normal range and warfarin to keep me from clotting. None of this affects how I live my life, with the exception of putting me at risk for heavy bleeding.

When the paramedics arrived at the scene of the accident, my medic alert bracelet denoted my blood condition and led them to know to give me vitamin K immediately to start getting my blood to coagulate. However, my condition also led me to bleed seriously as a result of the accident.

What I know of what happened is through what others have relayed to me. I was feeling on top of the world as I drove along, nearing home, when someone came out of a side street onto the highway and drove into the passenger side of my car. The impact pushed and turned my car into the oncoming traffic and I was hit again – t-boned on the driver's side. People told me later that they were either delayed for hours, or re-routed, getting home from work. An acquaintance was in a car three cars behind the one that t-boned me. She saw it all and filled me in later with eye-witness details.

The paramedics had to cut the top off my car to get me out. It was pouring rain. The flip charts I was to type up for my client were ruined, but my suitcases and computer survived. My magic facilitator wand (a multi-colored feather duster covered in gifts from workshop participants over my many years of facilitating) was bent, but could be used again.

Meanwhile at home, Joan had prepared dinner and was wondering where I was. Worried, she began calling hospitals and found the one where I had just been brought into emergency. She suffered a very big hit with this news. All they could tell her was that I had just arrived. They couldn't tell her what had happened. Their only guidance was to have someone drive her to the hospital, where they would have a social worker ready to speak with her.

At first, the medical practitioners weren't sure whether I would survive. Joan spent many hours by my side, answering the questions that I didn't even know I was asking. *Where am I? What happened?* She made all of the medical decisions that I couldn't make, including the call to put a titanium nail in my crushed left femur, even if the other injuries made the surgery very risky. The titanium nail went in and the bone healed around it.

As I lay in the hospital bed several days after the accident, unable to move or speak, the immediate gift of my hit began to surface. I became aware of a deep feeling of happiness that I was alive, and that I was meant to be alive to continue the work that I do.

Joan supported me all the way through my healing journey of six weeks in hospital and several months of concentrated rehabilitation. Out of this experience, and stemming from my awareness and happiness, she and I developed a model called *Being Authentically ALIVE*, which applies Appreciative Inquiry (AI) through challenging times in our personal and work lives. ALIVE is an acronym for *Appreciate, Love, Inquire, Venture and Evolve*. Appreciative Inquiry is an energizing approach for sparking positive change by engaging people in focusing on what is working well (appreciative), through asking questions and telling stories (inquiry). This focus allows people and organizations to build futures based on their strengths and successes in order to achieve their goals. AI is both a world-view and a process for facilitating positive change in human systems (individual, group, organization, community). Its assumption is simple: every human system "Has something that works right – things that give it life when it is most alive, effective, successful, and connected in healthy ways." (Cooperrider, Whitney, Stavros, 2003, p. xvii). AI begins by identifying this positive core and connecting to it in ways that heighten energy, sharpen vision, and inspire action for change. Since the 1980s, AI has been used to bring about collaborative and strengths-based change in communities and organizations worldwide. I've been using AI since 2001 in both my daily practice and in my work. Given this context, it is easy to see why I would draw upon AI in a time of challenge.

The gift from my hit was an opportunity to live what I teach about using AI. As a result of living it, my presenting, facilitating, consulting, writing, and teaching practices deepened for myself and for those participating in my work. And, an enormous gift was placing a priority on co-authoring with Joan our book, *Appreciative Inquiry In Higher Education: A Transformative Force*, which includes ALIVE as well as many other AI practices to share with the world. We have used and lived this model, making it easy to do workshops to help others to do the same.

Writing about my accident for our book was not easy, as the traumatic stress left me with anxiety. In time, I found ways to move along the emotional healing journey, as well as the physical healing journey.

Life is full of challenges, big or small. The ALIVE model came out of a very personal challenge. As we share our experience with others, it provides for them a framework for reflecting on the challenges in their work lives and their personal lives. The following is the reflective exercise that can be used to consider living through challenging times.

Reflective Practice Exercise

Imagine some of the challenges that you may have lived through in your work or personal life.

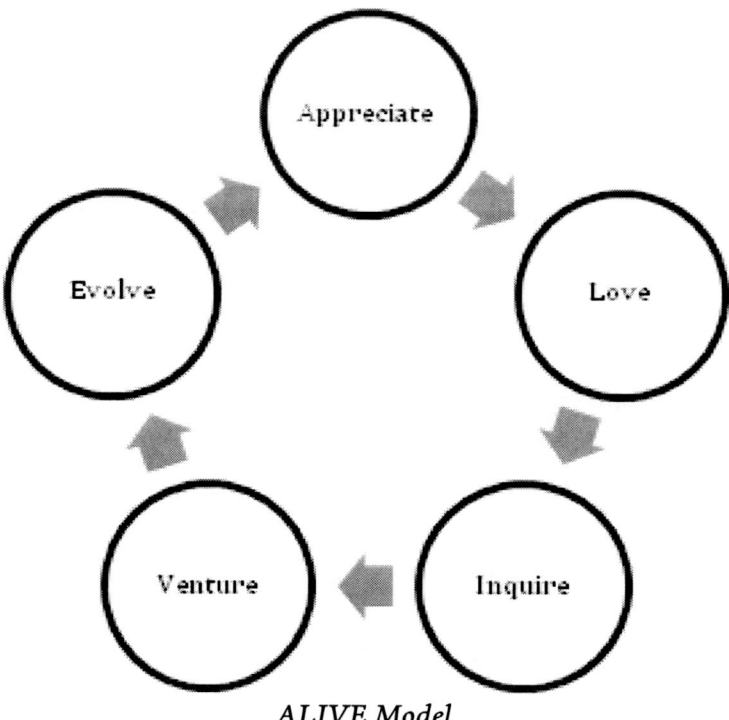

ALIVE Model

Apply the being authentically ALIVE model to your world through the following reflective questions:

- How have you lived through challenging times? Your challenge may not have been a life-threatening accident. No matter how big or small your challenge was, the reflective questions here are designed to help you think through how you were authentically ALIVE through the challenge. The result of living through the challenge may or may not have been a success.

- What did you learn, and how did this contribute to your evolution?

Following are some definitions and reflective questions for each of the five aspects of the ALIVE model. Some of them may fit your challenge, and some may not. Other questions may arise for you as you reflect on how you successfully lived through the challenge. Start with the part of ALIVE that you are drawn to and move through the parts that draw you as you reflect on living through your challenge.

Appreciate – value, increase in value, grasp the significance of, be fully aware of, express gratitude

- What did you value about the situation, yourself and others?

- What did you want more of?

- What were you fully aware of?

- What did you choose to focus on?

- How did you reframe to see the positive possibilities?

- How did you express gratitude?

- How did you seek and multiply appreciative moments?

Love – deeply care for yourself and others, be open and present with others, be loved and cared for by others

- How did you seek and recognize allies and supporters?

- How did you respond to their support?

- How did you and they show love?

- How were you open and present within these caring relationships?

- How did you care for yourself?

Inquire– ask questions, be curious, seek to learn, research, engage in dialogue

- What questions did you ask?
- How did you seek to learn about this situation?
- What did you learn?
- How did you engage with others?
- How did you reframe the situation to see possibilities?
- How did you strive to understand the outcomes outside of your control?

Venture – undertake, show courage, brave the risks

- How did you brave the storm?
- How did you courageously undertake to move forward?
- How did you find the courage and determination to follow expert advice?

Evolve – develop, unfold, expand, open

- How did you develop, unfold yourself into your future?
- What allowed you to expand and be open to opportunities?
- How have you incorporated the new and different you into your life, which is both the same and forever changed?
- (Cockell & McArthur-Blair, 2012, p. 87-88)

In my practice of reflective journaling, this ALIVE model is a framework for me to work through challenges in my life. Here, I illustrate with reflections on my car accident in each of the parts of ALIVE. In reflecting, I choose to focus on some aspect of the definitions and questions for each part.

Appreciate

When I first woke up in the hospital bed, I was aware (though not fully) that I wasn't able to move or speak. These were the things I couldn't do.

I asked myself what was it I *could* do. I could smile. This illustrates one of the key aspects of Appreciate – the ability to reframe to what is possible, rather than what is not possible. I was also very grateful to be alive. Gratitude is an important way to appreciate. As I continued along the slow healing journey, I appreciated what I could do each day. I appreciated being able to take a first step, then a second, eventually moving from using a walker to crutches, to a cane, and eventually to walking unsupported. All of these steps were based on appreciating what I could do.

Love

Love was a very significant part of my healing journey. Joan made sure that I not only had her love, but also the love of friends and family. Joan made sure people came to visit, sent me e-mails, etc. I was well loved. In the hospital, I was surrounded by gifts, cards and a large board of photos of people holding a big sign that said "Jeanie Rules," put together by my daughter. I was cared for very well by nurses, doctors, physiotherapists and other health care professionals. Their caring approach helped me to venture forward each day. I cared for myself, reflecting on what I was accomplishing each day and celebrating that. I cared for those I around me. I loved listening to people's stories, whether they were other patients in my ward, visitors or health care professionals.

Inquire

Daily, I asked what could I do? At first, I couldn't read or do Sudoku (one of my favorite pastimes). A friend would bring me daily Sudoku puzzles. I would just move the numbers around, though each day, I could do a little more. Eventually, I was back to my usual skill level. The same thing happened with reading. At first, I wasn't able to read. Soon, I was back to full reading capability. Each day I would ask myself, "What can I do today?" When the physiotherapists first suggested I would move out of the bed to using a walker, nine days after the accident, I inquired as to whether they were sure I could do that. They said that the surgeon had said I could put weight on my right leg because the pelvic breaks on that side were stable. So I started with one step, moving on to two steps the next day, and so on. Five weeks after the accident, I visited the surgeon to review my x-rays. He looked very surprised that my bones had healed so quickly. On returning to the rehab hospital for physiotherapy, my physiotherapists were also surprised when I said I could put full weight on both legs. They insisted the student physiotherapist inquire further by reading the surgeon's report. That inquiry led me to venture forward to beginning to use both legs.

Venture

As illustrated above, the first three parts of ALIVE – appreciate, love, inquire – help us to venture forward, try something new, and move ahead through the challenges. In my case, this meant moving ahead through my healing journey. Venturing beyond the hit required resilience and courage. I trusted the medical professionals who cared for me as I ventured forward. I felt that the physiotherapists were very appreciative as they encouraged me daily to try to do more. They set goals, such as to walk from the bed to the wall. At first, when I got only part way, they rewarded me with words of praise and hope that the next day I could try again.

Evolve

Through all my life hits – the blood disorder, cancer, car accident and lesser hits we all experience – I have kept on going. Fundamentally, my hopeful view of life has allowed me to live very successfully and fully through these times. Living through challenges such as the hit of a car accident, one is never the same as before. I am different in body, mind and spirit. My body has healed, but it still bears the results of being crushed. My mind deeply understands fear and my spirit understands that death is always close by each of us. Through the journey, one evolves into new ways of being – forever changed. This journey can be lived with joy or with sorrow. It is a choice that can influence how one lives when the outcome is not known. It may turn out good or bad, and one may live or die. Living with Appreciative Inquiry as a daily practice requires conscious effort and focus.

Today, I'm very much alive and well after a deeply personal healing journey grounded in my practice of Appreciative Inquiry, supported throughout by Joan. Lots of gifts have happened along our healing journeys. Joan and I now work together consulting, facilitating, speaking, writing, helping people and organizations to surface what's working well, and to build on that and become even better. We call this *Making Magic – facilitating futures not yet imagined.*

As I continue to live and evolve – practicing being authentically ALIVE – by speaking and writing authentically about who I am, I am living in the revolutionary last third of my life. I am confident in the wisdom I have gained through many successes and challenges. This wisdom allows me to be confident in speaking and writing, telling my stories and sharing my ideas boldly and confidently. I see more clearly the uniqueness and value of all people and the need to work towards a fairer world for all. The ALIVE model is a way to work through the challenges we face, especially when the path forward is not clear. It is not about changing outcomes that we can't control; it is about journeying in a way that grasps the most powerful moments of strength and builds upon them.

References

Cockell, J. & McArthur-Blair, J. (2012). *Appreciative Inquiry in Higher Education: A Transformative Force.* San Francisco, CA: Jossey-Bass.

Cooperrider, D., Whitney, D., Stavros, J. (2003). *Appreciative Inquiry Handbook: The First in a Series of AI Workbooks for Leaders of Change.* San Francisco, CA: Berrett-Koehler Publishers, Inc.

About Jeanie

BIO:

Dr. Jeanie Cockell, Co-President of Cockell McArthur-Blair Consulting, is an educational and organizational consultant. She specializes in collaboratively designing strategies to surface the wisdom of individuals and groups in order for them to build positive futures and to respond effectively to change. Her consulting practice is grounded in her education background including teaching and leadership roles. She is a dynamic facilitator who is known for her creativity, sense of humor, sensitivity, and ability to get diverse groups to work collaboratively together. She is a leader in Appreciative Inquiry as an organizational development process, a research methodology and a foundation for living well. She travels worldwide to facilitate workshops, speak at conferences, and consult for clients. Jeanie is an established author who has published articles, co-authored the book, *Appreciative Inquiry in Higher Education: A Transformative Force* (available on Amazon) and is working on another book, *Appreciative Resilience.*

Contact: jeanie@cockellmcarthur-blair.com

Website: www.cockellmcarthur-blair.com

Dr. Jeanie Cockell

Corey Poirier

HIT:

Confused and angry as a nine-year-old, it was easy to blame and target his mother as a scapegoat for their hardship, and his anxiety and hypochondria that followed her decision to divorce.

GIFT:

Being the sole focus of his single mothers devotion and love through thick and thin inspired Corey to pay it forward and devote his talents and time to help others to find and fulfill their unique passion and purpose.

Uncovering Lessons Through the Anxiety of Divorce

− *COREY POIRIER*

In a time when divorce has become so common, being the product of a divorce may not seem like a major hit. We all handle emotions differently though, and as an only child, and I was in love with the idea of my parents staying together forever. My father was my hero and my mother was my rock. I liked our little family.

As a child, having my hero and my rock in the same house, and growing up in gentle Prince Edward Island, life was good. I didn't feel life needed to change. Yet, despite my hopes and dreams at the time, life did change.

I was just nine years old when divorce happened, and it was nowhere near as common as it is today. I didn't see my parents fighting, and I wasn't old enough to understand the importance of being with a person who makes your heart sing, versus continuing to live with someone you fight with regularly.

Most of my extended family was comprised of couples, the majority of whom had been together for years. The idea that my family would be the only one in my circle that was a split family was difficult to accept.

My mother had already once decided to try and get back together with my father after a short split (that I didn't realize had really even happened). They had reunited mainly for my sake, though she had reached a point where she couldn't keep living what she felt was a lie.

At the time, I blamed my mother for the divorce, because she was brave enough to end what I thought was a healthy relationship. As a result of the decision, the amount of time I would spend with my father was reduced. Even when he failed to pick me up for our regular Sunday visits time after time, I still found a way to blame my mother. Even if I was just a child, it took me far longer than it should have to realize that my mother wasn't the *bad guy*.

What complicated the sting of the divorce was that sometimes we didn't have any groceries and could barely find something to eat for supper. Once, we had to use collectable coins to buy ourselves supper until my mother received her weekly paycheque. At the time, I had no awareness of how humiliating it must have been for her to go through this. I just thought, *well, you put us in this situation!* I now realize how unfair that was of me.

My hit came when the divorce initially occurred and the split of our family began, and it continued as I realized my father's part in the situation. Recognizing that your hero isn't all you think they are can be a tough pill to swallow.

The divorce impacted my schooling in various ways. I became the class clown, or at least the guy looking for extra attention I didn't feel I was getting in comparison to when I had my father and mother under the same roof. My choices had me acting out in various ways at school, getting detentions, getting called to the principal's office, and even getting in trouble with the law... albeit, in much smaller ways when compared to the more serious crime occurring in town. I was in trouble just the same.

I think my search for attention also influenced the type of friends I reached out to at the time, which in turn circled right back to more trouble with the law. My attention seeking didn't always result in the best of decisions, but sometimes attention is just that, attention.

The hit of the divorce became 'the hit that kept on giving.' My lingering situation of not understanding why my father didn't want to be more active in my life and not having closure in relation to my parents' split continued. Even being aware of the multitude of gifts from the hits in our lives, I don't think it's any surprise that the unresolved emotional issues we experience as children continue into our adult lives. As the sting of the hit continued for years, I believe it played at least some part in my emotional battles with anxiety and hypochondria.

Proving it was a hit that kept on giving, my anxiety saw me spending multiple days each work week in doctor's offices, hoping just *one* doctor could eventually determine what was going on with my physical health. At the time, I didn't realize my symptoms were the manifestations of my emotional struggles.

Week by week, my physical symptoms would vary. One week, I would experience tremors, the next a rapid heart rate, and then it could manifest as restless legs. A new symptom seemed to develop each time I went online to trying diagnose myself. I would read into the lists of possible symptoms of the potential illness I thought I had on any given week, never once realizing that my illness itself was hypochondria. I had the belief in a physical illness that didn't exist in the first place. Yet, I never once realized that was why no doctor could identify my illness.

Emotionally, I was a wreck, but didn't realize just *how much* of a wreck, because the symptoms were showcasing themselves physically. While I realized that not all of my anxiety was a result of my parent's divorce, but once I finally started doing some inner work, I saw that not having my father's presence in my life after having such a doting father in my earlier years, played a bigger part than I ever realized at the time.

It wasn't until my anxiety reached a boiling point in my mid-twenties that I finally started searching for some answers. That was when I was enlightened by multiple people, who shared that not having my father in my life in an active way may have triggered some of these emotions. I didn't do the required inner work all at once, but I paced myself and over time, I began to incorporate healing strategies such as practicing yoga, meditating, receiving Reiki treatments, and visiting and taking part in First Nation sweat lodge traditions. It was during the sweat lodge traditions where I finally spoke about my unresolved issues.

Truth be told, the greatest healer was undoubtedly uncovering my passion and purpose – that was the gateway to my gaining some control over, and ultimately, dissipating, in large part, both my anxiety and hypochondria. I'm not saying that what I did will be the answer for everyone, but most of the practices I welcomed into my life certainly wouldn't do anyone much harm. My peace with the hit came after I started living *on purpose*.

The Gifts

It was in my mid-teens, well before the anxiety hit a boiling point, I had finally begun to see the gift received as a result of what I felt was a major hit at the time. The gift unfolded gradually, in the form of the life lessons I began learning from my single mother, as we shared life together throughout my childhood and teen years. Her immeasurable gift came partly by example and partly by instruction. As I look back, several circumstances exhibited this very clearly.

The first came during the time when my mother had used collectable coins to buy us supper. Even then, I learned a life lesson, albeit unconsciously. I learned that people are more important than materials, and actions are more important than words.

The second clarity of my mother's gifts was tied to our pets. We always had a lot of pets – typically three dogs at a time. Sometimes, I felt as though they ate better than us. My mother has always favorite animals, probably because of the unconditional love they provide. As much as she loved them, she demonstrated sacrifice to me regularly in relation to our pets. She always maintained, and ultimately proved, that should one of them attack me, unprovoked, that she would take action, regardless of how much she loved them.

When I was eight years old, our dog, Lobo, bit my face. I was still a child and didn't provoke the attack, though I will always have a scar on my face to remember that day. Lobo was so cute and I didn't want to lose him. I fought my mother on the idea of putting him down. She too loved Lobo, and also didn't like the idea of putting him down, but she explained to me that once he attacked me the way he did, it would be common for him to attack again. Losing a favorite dog was hard, but I know now that my mother demonstrated true sacrifice for someone who is so partial to animals.

Another major lesson occurred when a classmate who had the same jacket as me took mine home instead. My jacket was brand new and his was in rough shape. Even though mine had my name written inside it, he still took it home 'by accident,' and never mentioned it afterward. Surely he knew the jacket wasn't his. I showed my Mom the ragged jacket and noted that we should contact his parents or the school to explain the mistake and make the exchange. My mother knew the child and his parents, and knew that he didn't have it easy. She explained that he probably needed the jacket more than me. (This was in spite of the fact that it wasn't long before this that we weren't able to afford groceries.) I noted that I didn't want to wear the rough looking jacket to school because people might recognize it was his; and yet, it was winter in Canada and I needed a winter jacket to wear.

My mother promised that we would find a way to get a new jacket, even though *my* new jacket was walking around with a classmate. Sure enough, I had a new jacket the very next day. I'm not sure how she got me that jacket, but her action came part and parcel with another life lesson: the most important time to give is often when it's hardest, or when it hurts the most to do so.

That classmate and I actually became decent friends, and remained so throughout the years. Such an unfolding wouldn't have happened had my mother agreed with my idea of calling his parents and embarrassing them by asking for him to exchange jackets the next day.

My mother also taught me about the importance of supporting those in your life. Anytime I had a new dream or mentioned wanting to try something new, she was the last person to say I shouldn't try something new, or that I should try to become more focused. When I was twelve, I decided I wanted to play guitar. Most of my family and friends felt I would never stay with it. I was an only child, and my grandmother admittedly spoiled me. As a result, I sometimes abandoned things quite quickly and easily. Whether it be a new video game, a new video system, a drum set, or the motor go-cart my father bought me after he and my mother had separated, I typically moved from one shiny object to the next. When I declared I wanted to play guitar (and perhaps be a musician or rock star someday), most of my family, rightfully, felt it was just another fleeting endeavor on my part. They concluded that as soon as I realize how much your fingers hurt when you began playing, or that your fingers can even bleed during practice (turns out the related Bryan Adams line in "Summer of 69" is accurate), I would toss the guitar aside like yesterday's news.

Hearing my dreams, my mother demonstrated unconditional support. She handed me her old guitar, a music lesson book, and reached out to my uncle Bobby to ask him to teach me my first chords. The result was that I stayed with guitar, despite small breaks throughout the years, and went on to record four CDs, have my music in rotation on radio, play hundreds of shows in venues across the country, release a music video, and even have my latest album get nominated for *Rock Recording of the Year*. My mother's support was so important during those early years. Her belief in me was unrelenting.

I believe my mother's support gave me the confidence to tackle many of my major fears, including the early fear I had in association with my career. I am a Motivational, Educational and Keynote Speaker, and I don't believe it would have been possible had my mother told me over and over all of the things I *couldn't* do, or that my dreams were too far-fetched.

Even when, in the middle of a successful corporate career in my late-twenties, I told my mother that I planned to switch to speaking, she never once said, "I don't really think that's a good idea."

The life lessons my mother provided during those impressionable years extended to include smaller life lessons as well. For instance, when I decided that I wanted to get my first car and also started smoking, she explained that she would buy my necessities, but was not prepared to pay for me to drive around smoking in my car. She said that I would need to get a job if I wanted to pay for a car and the cigarettes I thought I needed.

Unlike many of my friends whose parents forbade them from working a part-time job and smoking, I started working from a young age and also quit smoking at a young age as well. My mother taught me this indepen-dence. She also made me responsible for doing my own laundry, and if I wanted expensive name brand clothing, she would pay the portion that was equal to regular priced clothing and I would be responsible for the difference. I truly feel these actions taught me more responsibility at a young age then I ever could have learned otherwise.

My father didn't have a big presence in my life, or deliver as many life lessons, but my parents' break-up was the reason these gift (lessons) were possible in the first place. It admittedly still hurts knowing that I never got to throw a baseball or learn to drive a car with my father. It's also sad knowing my mother had to do basically all of the work by herself. It pains me that my grandfather lost one of his best friends when my mother and father went their separate ways; but out of these situations, the ones that did or didn't happen, new situations took their place. My grandfather found other friends whom he may not have had had my father still been in his life, and I developed a relationship with my grandfather, who took on a father-figure role for me. My mother and grandfather helped fill the void left by my father.

The gifts from my hit have truly never stopped. To this day, I still learn lessons from my mother and we have a very close mother-son relation-ship. We tell each other that we love one another during each phone call or message. We support one another in our endeavors. We seek each other's opinions regularly. And today, she and my girlfriend are also very close.

In my relationship with my girlfriend, I can see that the lessons my mother taught me continue to enhance my life. I feel the way I view my girlfriend, and how I treat her in our relationship, stem back to my learn-ing and witnessing how hard it can be for a female in a male-dominated world. I also feel my mother's example as taught me a lot about having respect for the women in one's life, and women in general.

How I interact with the people who enter my life, how I view the impor-tance of relationships, and even how I raise my own pets, all happened because of the hit I received at nine years of age. I couldn't have known it at the time, but it was such an important turning point in my life. It has shaped the person I have become so heavily that I can't imagine how different my life would be had I not experienced that hit.

I can't imagine not having all of the gifts I have received in the years since. I can't imagine my life being any more blessed and I wouldn't, for all of the money in the world, trade places with that kid back then if I knew he wouldn't go through that hit. I'm not advocating divorce or wishing it upon anyone, or stating that a child going through divorce will have the same experiences I had, but my hit was such an important part of my growth. I know it was the path I was meant to take.

Today, as a Keynote Speaker, Radio Show Host, Author, and even a Stand-up Comic, I see how the experiences I had during those years prepared me for my career in a way I couldn't have been prepared had I not gone through them. I can even recognize how the experiences have worked their way into my key message: that you need to step outside your comfort zone and uncover your passion if you want to become the best version of yourself.

When I interview people for our radio show, one of the key questions I ask them is, "If you were able to go back in time and sit across from a younger version of yourself at a pivotal point in your life, and give them one piece of advice, what would it be?" To demonstrate that I wouldn't take back one experience, if I was answering that question myself with all of this in mind, I would go back and say to that nine-year-old me: "It may hurt now, and it may seem like the end of the world, but you are going to be a better person for having taken this journey. This journey will give you so many life lessons that in essence, and your life would be for the worse were you not to be hit by this experience."

I may not use that exact wording, as my nine-year-old self might not get it, but I would essentially re-iterate that he needs to let the journey take its course, and not try to change it or feel he has to change anything. It will all work out the way it is meant to because in this case, *the journey became the destination.*

By going through the experience of divorce, I learned more about what it takes to be an active parent than I might have otherwise learned. I gained a forgiveness for my father that I may not have had, had things happened in a different way. I even gained an appreciation for the lessons he taught me. I have incorporated the many life lessons learned through my hit into my career and life. Reflecting on these lessons is a constant reminder of how I want to live my life and serve others. As a professional speaker, being responsible for your actions and yourself, being willing to make sacrifices (for your clients), knowing what to do and what not to do in life, knowing how to adapt to unexpected and tough situations, and giving even when it may hurt, are all lessons that serve me well, and serve anyone well.

My hit certainly taught me as much about any other hit in my life, including my battle with anxiety and hypochondria. For that reason, I feel it is every bit as significant. To that end, I hope any hit you may be forced to suffer through reveals just as many gifts for you.

About Corey

BIO:

From growing up in the Canadian Maritimes, to traveling through North America to speak to audiences small and large, Corey Poirier is an award-winning keynote speaker who has presented to over 100,000 attendees and shared the bill with Deepak Chopra, Stephen M.R. Covey, and General Rick Hillier. He is the host of the top-rated *Conversations with PASSION* radio show, which has featured Jack Canfield, John Gray, Rick Hansen, Olympic Gold Medalist Silken Laumann, Turbo Jam Creator Chalene Johnson and hundreds more.

Corey is also an International Best-Selling Author who has presented at TEDx and MoMondays. He is the founder of a business publication, a nine-time acclaimed and best-selling author, and the CEO of a seminar and media company that has interviewed more than 3000 super-achievers. He is a seasoned stand-up comedian and a *Rock Recording of the Year* nominee.

Websites: www.thatspeakerguy.com
       www.thepassioncure.com

Corey Poirier

Ella-Fay Zalezsak

HIT:

Ella-Fay questioned how she could bury the life that she had been building with her husband when he suddenly passed away, leaving her with mounting bills, a pre-teen son, a teenage daughter and a broken heart.

GIFT:

With evolving strength, spirit and courage, Ella-Fay opened her life to a path of friends and a wealth of experience that led her to discover her authentic self and happiness.

Planting Seeds for Renewed Joy

— *ELLA-FAY ZALEZSAK*

Life wasn't all roses. It was hectic, full and demanding. It was hard being a mother of two children and working two jobs to make ends meet. I felt as though I was continuously running on overtime, as the primary wage earner and provider for our family. As I worked tireless days and nights, Otto, my husband, was desperately trying to find work. Doors kept closing before him. He hated the menial jobs he took, settling for minimum wage, with memories of his once well-paying opportunities of stable employment. His free spirit couldn't tolerate the confinement of the office, until life squeezed him into accepting whatever he could get. He had settled for trickles of part-time hours in places he didn't want to be. We were in survival mode.

The kids were dealing with their own typical daily life adventures, stresses at school, puberty, and interpersonal dynamics that, at times, became challenging conflicts to their ability to cope and handle things. Through the chaos, there were peaceful aspects to our lives as well – we had a lovely garden and a wonderful dog that soothed the more hectic moments and kept the kids busy rolling in laughter. Otto and I were careful not to give away our frustrations, but they were difficult to contain to times when the kids were out. We knew they were aware that something was up, but were never really sure of what it was. As far as they were concerned, everything looked normal.

When Otto and I had met, we had envisioned a life of building shared goals of home and family, annual vacations, and a relatively stable life.

While we were committed to our common dreams, life was coming at us full force. We were seldom finding time for quality moments of sharing, relaxing or loving life. A romantic getaway for us involved a quick trip to Tim Hortons for a cup of coffee, or a late night stroll to gaze at the stars, walk the dog and discuss how to handle all that was going on. We were drained by worry, work and all of the bills coming our way. How we got to such a place was a mystery to me. It was so distant from what we had agreed to before we got married.

Our financial strains were contributing to building of walls between us… and yet, the love we shared could just as easily crumble those walls. It was perhaps much like many aspects of our lives: crumbling one minute and rebuilding the next. We threw the words of divorce around as we quarreled over how to handle the bills, yet neither of us could take the first drastic step in separating. The truth was that we loved each other, and we loved our children too much to take that path. There was no denying that daily living was taking a toll on the both of us. I was exhausted and couldn't possibly take on a third job in addition to my full time and part-time positions… all the while raising two beautiful children. It didn't seem fair. Worst of all, the loving intimacy Otto and I had shared so intensely in the not so distant past was slowly dying.

That was the week that everything changed. It was Wednesday night, after another exhausting day of being challenged to the maximum. Something different was in the air. For whatever reason, neither Otto nor I had the energy to raise our voices. Instead, we decided to turn to each other for comfort. Something inside us was propelling us to be kind to each other. We shared a sweet evening of great delight, as we felt memories of our first time together rush forward. Those few hours shared were beautiful, loving and tender, ending in a gentle drift into relaxed sleep, curled up together.

From hours of satisfying sleep, I awoke startled by the sudden bright sting of the bedroom lights blaring into my eyes and Otto trying desperately to tell me something. What was going on? What was he saying? I couldn't grasp his words. It finally became clearer. He was telling me he felt sick.

A sense of numbing panic washed over my body as I sat in total confusion. Who should I call? What was happening? I raced to phone and called the hospital. The person on the other end advised that I give my husband Gravol. I wanted to jump out of the phone at her and scream "Are you hearing me?" Attempting to retain my rationality, I told her that my husband was turning grey. I slammed the phone down to disconnect the line and frantically dial 911.

"Please send help!" I remember saying.

"Oh no, he's having a seizure," I screamed.

As the 911 attendant tried to assist me, I yelled my address out. I hung up the phone and ran to Otto. Within minutes the fire department arrived. They placed an oxygen mask on him, as they reassured me that he was just in need of a little assistance. As they tended to him, I became aware that I would need to get dressed and get to the hospital with him. The ambulance soon arrived and the fireman described what was happening on my behalf, before the ambulance attendant told me that they are taking my husband to the hospital.

A million thoughts invaded my clarity of thinking. As I tried to gather myself to follow the ambulance, my daughter came rushing down the stairs asking what all the noise was about. I started to tell her that Daddy wasn't feeling well, and that he had been taken to the hospital. Knowing I had to ensure my insulin-dependent diabetic daughter was okay before I left, I checked her sugar levels. The hospital was a mere ten minutes away, so I could check on Otto and be back quickly if she needed me. In the meantime, I urged her to go back to sleep, since it was a school night. I gave her some juice, got dressed and raced off to the hospital.

When I arrived, the attending doctor informed me that they needed to stabilize Otto and that I would have to wait in the side room. I was numb, tired and not connecting to what was happening. As I sat alone, a nurse dropped by and asked me if I had a friend who could be with me. It was 3:00 a.m. and everyone was sleeping. Was she nuts? I replied with a simple no, and asked when I could see my husband.

Why couldn't I see my husband? What was going on? Without delivering an answer to my urgent question, the nurse simply left. I sat there dumbfounded, only to notice that she had quickly returned.

"Do you have a minister that could come and sit with you?" she asked.

Why do I need a minister? I thought. What a weird question! I simply replied no once again and reiterated my earlier question as to when I could see my husband. Again, she walked away leaving me in the small silent space, without any answers. I felt brain dead and tired, wishing only for Otto and I to go back home. I was worried about my kids, even though I knew they were fast asleep.

A strange, kindly man of the cloth then came in and sat down next to me. I was oblivious as to why he was there. He had a bible with him. He looked like he was praying. I wondered if there was another emergency in the hospital and he was waiting to see someone.

The same nurse returned once again. This time she didn't come with questions. She stared me in the face.

"I am sorry, but your husband has passed away," she said.

I just stared at her mouth. What did she just say?

"Your husband has died. Do you have someone you can call?"

I stared at her in disbelief and muttered "My godmother," as I sunk to the floor.

All I could think was this couldn't be happening. They must be mistaken.

When I mustered the strength to call my godmother, she knew something awful had happened ... otherwise, I wouldn't have been calling just after 3:00 a.m.

"What is happening? Are you okay?" she asked.

"No", I replied. "I am at the hospital. Otto has died."

"What?" she exclaimed.

"Otto died. Can you come to the hospital?" I asked.

Fortunately, she lived less than ten minutes away and agreed to come immediately. I told the nurse that my godmother was on her way, as I collapsed in uncontrollable tears. The minister sat there praying, as he reached out to comfort me.

He has died echoed in my ears, but my brain couldn't grasp it. He was dead and I all I wanted to do was yell out *No, just let me take him home.* Oh God, I wanted us to go home together!

My godmother soon arrived with questions I couldn't answer. The nurse returned, asking if I wanted to see my husband. My godmother turned to me and said that she would come in with me. Finally, I got to see my husband, but he was only the body of my beloved.

As I touched him, the tears flowed. My mind was screaming out, *Don't leave me!* It was too late; he was already gone. *He's gone.* I trembled as the tears ran down my face. *He's gone.*

I had experienced a lot of knocks from life and had been able to get back up, but this hit penetrated me to the core. It rocked my emotional world, leaving me crippled. Otto was my confidant, my lover, and the person who came closest to understanding me. He was my husband, my every-thing… and he was gone.

My godmother drove me home and called my parents for me. I couldn't talk. The tears were flowing non-stop. I listened to my mom talk to me on the phone, letting me know that they would be at my home as soon as they could get there. My godmother assured me that she would stay until they arrived.

The hardest thing for me was to tell the kids when they came downstairs in the morning. My son reacted by going into hiding on the back porch with the dog curled up next to him. My daughter sat with me in the kitchen. Between 'Kleenex moments' and hugs, we choked on our words, unable to properly communicate about our dreadful reality. When I called my brother-in-law, he was in shock. For the first few hours of that early morning, all I did was cry, hug my kids and cry some more. I knew

Otto was dead, and yet, a part of me just wanted him to be alive and at home with us. Why was this happening?

Over the next few days, friends, family and neighbors came by to share their condolences. The school called and asked if they could hold a mass in memory of my husband. I agreed. The parish priest dropped by to see how I was doing and what could he help with. My insurance agent arranged a meeting time with the funeral home. My brother-in-law had to scoop me up by the arm and help walk me to the car to get to that appointment. I didn't want to do it. He was there with me, helping and guiding me through the toughest moments.

With the help and support of friends, I went through the motions of getting everything in place for the funeral. Father Cote – the priest from the parish school – was a God-send. The parish women put together refreshments for after the service. I hadn't even given it any thought. I focused on the service and what passages to read, and I translated a poem by my husband into English entitled, *Until We Meet Again*, to be read at the funeral. I was functioning enough to get done what was expected of me.

After the service, people gathered to help me say good-bye. We shared stories and even laughed over some warm memories. I was there, participating in body only.

As the days passed, I began spending longer hours in the shower, where I cried uncontrollably so as not to worry anyone. I wanted to be strong for the kids, but the truth was that I wasn't strong. I felt as though my world had ended with Otto's death. I was drowning in the flood of my tears. I became lost in the loss. I tried to hide my grief. I went to grief counselling, and made arrangements for the kids to attend as well. I buried myself in my work, as my income became even more vital for the well-being of our family.

I joined a bereavement group and met others on a similar path, each with their own painful story as to how loss was brought into their worlds. As we gathered together in the nine-week program, we all wanted to heal, though we weren't sure how. We were seekers looking for an anaesthetic to help us move on. Following the biblical references to the mustard seed, I began wearing a mustard seed pin. I had such little faith that things would get better during those heart-heavy times that the most strength I could muster up was only about as big as a mustard seed.

. . . . .

> When looking back on my first few years as a widow, I see them as my *zombie years*. I went through the motions of getting things done, though I felt fully disconnected from life. Each day, I would robotically complete tasks; and at night, I would be overcome by emotions. I lacked enthusiasm and I was missing joy. I was sad, angry and hurt. At times, I felt abandoned by my partner.

The next few years were tough, as I experienced the truth of the saying *When it rains, it pours*. Just as I would pass through another challenge, something else would veer its ugly head and daunt me. I felt my faith quiver, despite all the prayers. The rebellious teen years are difficult enough in regular circumstances, but as a single parent stuck in my own grief, they began to seem unbearable. I had a few health scares in the first year, followed by an accident. One slip on ice cost me a smashed ankle, three and a half hours of reconstructive surgery, and several months of physiotherapy. My mother's cancer resurfaced and her health was failing. She too needed my help. My father had a fall that caused permanent brain damage, and in order to ensure he was being looked after, I became his health advocate.

It was a full five years later when I decided that I was ready to bury my husband's ashes. My children agreed that it was time. After some searching, I found the perfect spot and arranged for our own ceremony. Each of us brought something we wanted to place in the ground with the ashes. During the ceremony, I read a letter aloud that I had written, as I spread Otto's ashes into the ground. If you were to ask what I wrote, I would honestly say that I can't remember. I poured my unspoken words onto paper and released them. I then buried the letter with his ashes. This act was the first step in the unfolding of a new journey for me. My children and I each did what was right for us that day, as we cried with the first genuine release of the grief we had been carrying. In that moment, we felt the world stand still. It felt as though the universe was helping us to release our pain.

Reflecting back on the sorrow, the challenges and all the events that followed Otto's death, I realized that the burying of his ashes, in a sense, became a planting of seeds for the gifts that followed. In fact, I would now say there were many blessings and gifts that enriched my life, all stemming from painful loss. I met the perfect friend who had never gotten over the passing of someone important to him. He was digging himself into rubble everywhere. Seeing him live with a closed heart made it apparent to me that I was doing the same.

On New Year's Eve, six years after my husband's passing, I made a commitment to myself to experience joy in my life. I resolved to fake it until I could make it real for myself. My life mantra became *I am Joy*, and in each and every year to come, I envisioned creating more joy than the year before. Having made that choice, people were placed on my path that became life-changing mentors, and I began to find myself again.

I met a motivational speaker who reminded me of the joy in laughter and how it could lighten the day. Slowly but surely, I began to laugh again. I met a spiritual teacher who lived life to the fullest and reminded me that she too was still learning and embracing life with play. Through her, I learned to accept myself as I was, with all that I was. I knew that at any point, I could change my mind and do something different, something new. I began trying new things with a sense of discovery, and from that point, every day seemed to lead to something new unfolding in my world.

I met a stranger who shared that every moment spent in sharing a kind word with someone added beauty to the world, and I chose to add beauty to my life. I began to want to open my heart to love, purely and joyfully.

With more joy and zest with every passing year, I began to live again. I took risks, had adventures, and even allowed myself to make mistakes. I watched myself grow and become more compassionate and real. Through the planting of all these seeds, I found my greatest gift: my authentic self. It was then that I received an amazing blessing.

A little blessed mentor entered my life – a granddaughter who exudes love with every breath, every smile, and every sweet uttering of the words *I love you Grandma*. This little mentor, Azriella, has flung my heart wide open and filled it with unimaginable joy. She helped confirm that I am finally at home within my own skin. Today, I am back to smelling the aroma of roses, feeling the mist by waterfalls, enjoying the melodies of birds chirping, and basking in awareness of the joyful laughter that surrounds me. I am content with life, and as my days unfold, I look for the hidden blessings. While loved ones have passed on and I miss them, I find something to rejoice about every day. I have discovered love in so many forms, and I am at peace with myself. I savour the blessings of the people in my life and I am grateful for the memories shared. The memories I create carry me through the challenging moments with strength and joy. I have opened my heart and learned to love life again. I have stepped into total acceptance that I can choose to be joyful. I am no longer lost in the loss, but found in the *now*, embracing life with joy.

I have come to the understanding that our greatest adversity – our hit from life – just might be the best catalyst to help us discover the depths of our own magnificence. It may be the coach that gets us to bring forth our own gifts to the world around us. This realization is the precious gift of my hit.

About Ella-Fay

BIO:

As a professional librarian, Ella-Fay Zalezsak has been committed to life-long learning. Recognizing that life is a continuous discovery process, she has resurfaced from a number of trying challenges. Her convictions helped her surpass these trials except for the biggest hit – the death of her husband, Otto. With faith as tiny as a mustard seed, she began a new journey into self-discovery.

Ella-Fay has travelled across Canada, relishing the unique qualities of living on both coasts. Today, she gives her love to many passions and hobbies, including writing and photography. She thrives in her adventures with granddaughter, Azriella, which lead to fun bedtime stories. She loves taking walks with her camera, experimenting in the kitchen, going out dancing and jumping the waves in a wave pool. Most of all, she loves teaching and helping others explore the world of information. Her daily commitment is to take pleasure enjoying the simple things in life and rejoicing in being her authentic self.

Email: ellafay@hotmail.com

Ella-Fay Zalezsak

Ken Pierce

HIT:

A sharp pain in his left arm pulled Ken back from his immi-
nent retirement and life as a vegetarian jogger psychologist.
It was a pain that uncovered the truth of heart disease and
a new life of being married to nature's laws.

GIFT:

Gaining awareness of the two sides of stress, Ken woke up
to the immaculate perfection of his life and gratitude for
not just its pleasures but equally its pains, regardless of
where they appear.

Equal Parts of Heaven and Hell

– *KEN PIERCE*

For over twenty years, I jogged daily, and was a fairly devoted vegetarian. I was five foot eight and one-hundred-and-forty pounds of lean muscle. Fifty push-ups were part of my daily routine. According to some, I looked at least ten years younger than my chronological age. I had regular check-ups with my longstanding family physician and took my vitamins faithfully. Beyond facing a mild asthma condition that was well under control, I was in good physical health. Everything seemed in line as I neared retirement after twenty-five years at the local community college. I also had a small private practice as a clinical psychologist, where I worked to try and save people from unhealthy lifestyles. And perhaps most importantly, I had a devoted spouse of thirty years with her own profession and three wonderful daughters, who were all doing well.

In late October of my retirement year, I got a pain down my left arm and immediately went to my doctor. Checking me over, he smiled and said that given my health history and overall condition, what I felt was probably just a muscle spasm. I remember him saying something to the effect, "Whatever you been doing, keep doing it, because it is working for you."

I went back to my life … until one evening three weeks later. I was walking with my wife when I had another pain down my left arm. She immediately dragged me to the nearby medical clinic. Once again, I was checked by an attending physician (whom I had never met before). She was thorough, like my regular doctor, but she differed in that she had no preconceived notions or medical history on me. After her examination, a very serious expression cast over her face and she handed me a prescription.

She said, "This is for nitro. Don't leave home without it! You don't fit the profile, but, you may have a blocked artery in your heart. Get to your own doctor tomorrow and have the tests to find out. Meanwhile, use the nitro anytime you experience those pains. Any questions Mr. Pierce?"

I was stunned, shocked and totally surprised! And then, I became angry... really angry! I assumed I had been doing all the *right* things to be healthy. I thought I had the evidence to prove I was doing all the *right* things! Now, I was being told they weren't the *right* things, and I was being treated for a condition that would typically be associated with someone who did little to take care of their health. What was going on?

Within twenty-four hours, I was parked in my regular doctor's office, waiting until he had an opening to see me. His nurse was very accommodating, and I was able to get in to see him within an hour.

Less than ten days later, I was in the heart surgery unit of the regional hospital, sitting across from the surgeon who planned on doing bypass surgery *on me*. Dr. Baxter was a friendly elderly man with a soft demeanor. He must have sensed that I was upset, because he was telling me that he was wearing his special *lucky shoes*. He only wore them when he did his surgeries. I looked down to see a pair of old, beat up brown loafers. I was not impressed. I couldn't help but think, *What the hell am I doing here? Why me? I'd been really good, hadn't I?*

My friendly new surgeon explained my two options were the insertion of a stent in the blocked artery, or replacing the artery with a bypass. He explained that the former was the preferred option, but if it didn't work, he (then he said, "we") had the latter, as a back-up plan. I found myself still unimpressed, and none too relieved by his attempts to comfort me. I think he saw me as both angry and despondent, which I was!

As we sat in the room, he added a heart-warming comment: "Hey Ken," he said, "Relax! You're a surgeon's dream!"

"A *surgeon's dream*?" I exploded at him, "What do you mean?"

"Ken, you're lean, and in general good health, so I can get in and out easily. If your health was poorer, or you were a person with extra mass, the surgery could present other challenges."

As I was wallowing in my good fortune of being easy to cut up, I realized this was also my opportunity to find out why I was there, in the first place. I decided to quiz the resident expert sitting in front of me.

"Dr. Baxter, why me? Why am I – a long-standing vegetarian jogger, who only pumps vitamins and iron, in hospital, in your cardiovascular ward?"

He smiled softly and said in a quiet voice, "You must think we know what are doing. Ken. We are only guessing half the time! We know a lot about how the human body works, but there's a lot more we don't know yet!"

He explained how even though medical tools and techniques were advancing every day, there was so much more yet to learn. He told me his cardiology unit sees more and more people every day who do not fit the heart disease stereotype of a passive lifestyle, excessive weight and poor nutrition. Then, he asked me the question that no self-respecting psychologist ever wants to be asked....

"Ken, how's your stress life?"

It was like he had sucker-punched me in the nose! And yet, Dr. Baxter's question was the most obvious question, and one I had ignored. It was the obvious question to ask, and the one that I was avoiding. I knew I needed to address it in order to have a future.

I frequently find myself missing the obvious – like the time I was looking for my glasses, and they were sitting above my forehead, or the time, I was looking for my car keys, and they were right in front of me on the kitchen counter. While I may have been looking for the answer behind what led me to be on the cusp of cardiac surgery, I hadn't really been seeing what was staring me in the face.

It all came together for me after this new insight struck. It all started to make sense. Growing up in a large, poor family, where we often struggled to make ends meet, I was left with the illusion that you could buy security, if you had enough money. I carried this belief through my life, and used it to guide my decisions on many occasions. I had forgotten what Helen Keller once said, "There is no security in nature, life is a daring adventure or nothing!"

The truth is there is no safety, or predictability, in our universe, except the laws of nature which we are constantly trying to uncover and understand. These laws of nature prevail constantly, and continuously, and determine all aspects of our life, and our future. If there were safety, the insurance industry wouldn't be one of the biggest industries on the globe.

If you pick any successful person who has roses by societal standards – fame, fortune, success – then you will also find manure in their story. It takes the fertilizer of manure to grow the roses. In the same way, it took the hit of my heart incident to draw my attention to my perfect life.

One of the most basic of nature's laws is the law of symmetry. This law, also called the law of balance, equilibrium or duality, states there are two sides to everything. It is a law reflected in our language with the dualities of good and bad, up and down, in and out, over and under, and so on. We see the principle in action in electrical systems with positive and negative charges, in our weather with high and low pressure systems, in our economy with bull and bear markets, and even in our marital relationships of optimists and pessimists creating the most stable relationships.

In biology, the symmetry law is called *homeostasis*. It is one of the fundamental laws in the human body. Our body constantly strives to maintain a balance, not just physically in its external design, but also, internally, at every level, right down to each individual cell. Even mentally, our mind is constantly seeking balance in some form. That's why we can't have a fantasy without a nightmare to motivate it, or vice versa. In theology, the law is reflected with each school of thought having some form of heaven and hell.

My hell was the fear and pain of heart disease. I had yet to uncover the other side. In honor of the truth of the natural law of symmetry, I was being motivated to notice and appreciate the divine: the *hellish heaven*, or *heavenly hell*, of heart disease.

As I opened myself to this exploration, I could see how the law of symmetry also applied to our health systems. We have often been told, by various experts, there is a *mind-body connection*. This is a myth! Our mind and body are one inseparable system. They are a system that follows the law of symmetry. When you go to your physician, you go to restore balance to some part of your system. We forget that our body is a self-healing system, and medical interventions are intended to encourage that process. Research has shown repeatedly that our thoughts and our beliefs affect this system at the level of our cellular structure, and our DNA. So, our thinking directly affects our health....

Consider the term *remission* in medical jargon. It occurs when a serious disease has suddenly, and unexpectedly resolved itself, with or without medical intervention. What is happening is implied in the word *remission* itself. Every health challenge we face demands that we *re-mission* our life, in alignment with the laws of nature. I was being given the opportunity to *re-mission* or re-design my life in keeping with my purpose and values, and natural laws.

I had been ignoring the obvious, again! I had been amiss to the law of balance in my life. While I was doing a number of things to promote my physical health, I was ignoring my mental health. The irony here, of course, is I was in the business of helping others to achieve mental well-being. You have probably heard it said that medical professionals make the worst patients, and here I was, a classic example.

I had spent the last five years at my job waiting for the security of a pension plan. I moved from one position to another biding my time, until I could get the *golden handshake*. I was under the illusion that my pension would ensure my future security.

To remind me of this illusion, and anchor the important learning, I was privileged to be laid off, just six months before my pension was to start. This, of course, further jeopardized my so called *security*, though it also cemented Helen Keller's priceless lesson in my mind and changed my life forever.

In my private practice, I have the privilege of working with individuals from age four to eighty-four, from the unemployed to multimillionaires, from jocks to palliative care patients. The work has given me the opportunity to notice how each and every person's life follows the law of symmetry. I reflected upon my four-year-old client being traumatized by the loss of her teddy bear, in the same way the eighty-four-year-old was traumatized by the loss of his health. I remember how the pain of the unemployed mother with the delinquent daughter was the same as the pain of the CEO with the daughter who wasn't interested in saving the family business.

We are hard-wired to seek pleasure and avoid pain. This is our dualistic learning system, which ensures our survival. In this journey, we get the experiences and relationships we need to ensure we learn what we need to learn, to grow in self-appreciation and self-confidence. It's a perfect system of counterbalancing pleasure and pain, at all times, in all places, for all people, in keeping with this divine law called symmetry.

Once we're born, we start dying, but in between, we get just the health challenges we need to ensure we learn to appreciate ourselves, our relationships and our life. I remember a client I had the privilege of working with who was a palliative care nurse. She said it was the perfect job for her. She told me people in palliative care have no enemies, and no friends! She elaborated further stating her patients appreciate any person who made time for them, loving every person in front of their face, without exception. Now that's real wisdom!

I had my surgery, and the stent worked. It still does to this day. Dr. Baxter told me after the surgery that the blockage was so situated, had I not been in such good physical shape, I probably wouldn't have survived the two initial angina attacks. So, there was no mistakes in all the previous things I had been doing. I just need to include my whole body – the mental and physical equally – going forward.

My recovery from the surgery was slow and arduous. I remember being black and blue from my nipples to my knees, looking like I had lost a bar fight...and badly. Those slow, quiet afternoons of recovery during those long winter months also gave me time to think, evaluate and most importantly, learn. I learned to trust my own spirit, above all else. I learned to appreciate my constant ability to learn, regardless of where or when. I learned to only do what I love, and that there is no time for anything else. I learned I was a billionaire, and I could find that kind of abundance easily if I simply looked, carefully. I learned who my real friends were, and to stop trying to make a difference in the lives of others, and start making a difference in my own. I learned what family really means, extending it far beyond being a biological relation. And I learned to appreciate each day, each breath and each movement I have the privilege to experience.

I came to the realization there is no retirement in nature; our true retirement is called death! I had to take care of my mind as well as I had my body. It became clear I had a specific purpose, which I had not been pursuing as the center of my focus. All along, I had been using my purpose as the frosting on the cake of my life, instead of the cake itself. When I was fully purposeful, my mind would be in as good a shape as my body. That was the task ahead.

Many people still believe there is a cure for cancer. To date, there are over two-hundred kinds of cancer. Depending on the type of cancer, treatments range from surgery to radiation, and chemotherapy to stems cells. Cancer is basically excessive cell mutation, which is a natural process enabling us to adapt quickly to our environment. I believe a cure for cancer is as big an illusion as world peace. Neither is achievable, because cancer and war each serve humanity in special and valuable ways. The internal conflict of cancer and the external conflict of war provide essential learning opportunities for us which contribute to the evolution and survival of our species.

Cancer kills about seven million of us annually, plus, millions of other mammals. It is one of the ways nature brings balance to excessive populations which endanger our planet's survival. So, it serves us physically as a species. But, what about mentally? I have had several clients over the years experiencing cancer in some form. They have each mirrored the best definition I have heard of the value of this disease: cancer is nature's last ditch effort to get a person to value themselves and their life.

The attitude of gratitude, frequently displayed by those experiencing cancer, is something we are all striving to learn in our own way. Since we all eventually get a short ride in a long hearse, it has been said by those wise elders around us: there are only five last words needed for the perfect death. Those words are: "Thank you. I love you."

When I was offered another job with good pay and benefits on the last day of my employment (a job which was not purposeful enough for my future), I gratefully and politely declined. I had finally learned my lesson, and Helen's lesson: *There's no security in nature, life is a daring adventure or nothing!*

Having security, in any form, is a common illusion, which is not available to anyone. Letting go of security opened me up to countless other truths. Since there are no mistakes in nature, so too there can be no mistakes in our life. Getting hit with my heart incident was my wake-up call – my opportunity to grow, survive, and extend the privilege of my life. It was one of the best things to have ever happen to me, in close company with my marriage, children and grandchildren.

Namaste. I salute the grandly organized design(er) of the universe manifested in you!

About Ken

BIO:

Ken Pierce – a board-certified psychologist – is an international speaker and author who holds Senior Faculty status with the Demartini Institute of Houston, Johannesburg and Sydney, and the Glasser Institute of Los Angeles. He has served on the faculty of Holland College and the University of Prince Edward Island. He is a Master Practitioner and Trainer in Neuro-Linguistic Programming and a Certified DACUM Facilitator.

Ken has worked for over thirty-five years in counselling, corporate and business coaching and education. He has published in several areas including business, *Using Lead Management on Purpose*, occupational analysis, *The DACUM Handbook*; education, *The Foundations of Early Childhood Education,* bullying, *The Dance of Bullying,* and health, *The Grandfather's Tale.*

Through his company, Clarendon Consulting, Ken provides individual and organizational transformation services to corporate clients while maintaining a counseling and coaching practice. His suite of offices and websites enable him to offer his services globally.

Websites: www.kenpiercepsychologist.com
www.mental-health-center.com

Ken Pierce

Jenny Kierstead

HIT:

Growing up with a family member with mental illness, Jenny survived her confusion, guilt and crippling self-esteem by clinging to the rigidity of perfectionism, which escalated into a life-threatening case of anorexia nervosa.

GIFT:

On the brink of starving to death, Jenny leapt into the unknown depths of her inner world, searching for her true essence beyond the suffering. Now a respected yogi and renowned spiritual teacher, she is the founder of a franchise system of yoga studios to *Awaken the Extraordinary* in others.

The Seeds of Nourishment
– JENNY KIERSTEAD

When I was sixteen years old, my whole world came tumbling down around me — my dream of becoming a university basketball player was in sudden jeopardy, my parents were divorcing, my dog was killed, my boyfriend was diagnosed with cancer, and my dear grandmother passed away. Any one of these occurrences would be considered traumatic, and I had all of them happen at once! It was indeed, the perfect storm.

Up until that point, my life had been status quo: the same house, same family structure, same routine and same friends. My parents were respected leaders in the community and my two siblings and I were well loved. People used to think of our family as the ideal; but behind our outwardly perfect image, there was a storm stirring that would eventually crest into a massive wave of destruction. And when it hit, I was completely ill prepared.

As I attempted to cling to the pieces of my crumbling world, I used what few coping mechanisms I had at the age of sixteen. I dealt with the perfect storm by controlling what aspects of life I could: my diet and my body. Before I realized what was happening, the dark power of anorexia had taken ahold of my life, and continued to do so for years. I lived with a desire to escape from being me, and the despair of knowing there was nowhere else to live.

The Seed of Disease

During my final year of high school, I decided I would play around with dieting for a few weeks. Although I was at a perfect weight for an athletic sixteen-year-old, I bought into the unrealistic standards shown to me in the media. What began as an innocent decrease of calories, exploded into a colossal loss of thirty pounds in just a few months. As my life was crashing down all around me, it was the only source of power I could grasp.

As my parent's relationship eroded, along with my sense of security, my addiction to perfection grew. And as my addiction to perfection grew, so did my anxiety and fear of failure. I stopped playing the sports I was mediocre in. I refused opportunities in school musicals. I became more obsessed with perfecting my performance in basketball. Before I knew it, my world had become very small, and very controlled. I had unconsciously misplaced my value as a person, handing it over to the scoreboard and peer approval.

When basketball season came to a close, I transferred my perfection addiction to my appearance, and went to work on sculpting the 'perfect body.' In attempts to achieve this, my life became even more contracted. I stopped swimming for fear that someone might judge my body. I stopped wrestling with my siblings for fear that my make up would smudge. I stopped singing for fear that I might slide out of key. Pretty soon, I had relinquished all sources of enjoyment in my life, in honor of perfection.

I'll never forget hearing my mother crying on the phone, as she called my sister, Lisa, to warn her about my condition before she returned home from an exchange in France. "She's just stopped eating," my mother said, "Some days we only see her eat an apple and rice cakes."

My body had become different. I was dangerously sick and mom knew it. Despite my diminishing physical strength, I was motivated by my weight loss. I was skinny and proud of it, viewing it as a great achievement. My self-discipline had become misdirected under the influence of diseased thinking.

By the time September came around, my life-long dream of playing university basketball was completely in jeopardy. As the top rookie recruit for the Acadia University women's team, I showed up at my first practice, only to be tossed around the court like a feather in the wind. That was my first and last practice with the Acadia team.

The Death Trap of 'Skinny'

After my first full year of university, I returned home to work as a day camp leader. One sunny afternoon in the comfort of home, I thought I'd push my edge and try some yogurt with raisins. As I poured the yogurt into the bowl, I felt heat rising from the pit of my belly and a quake of panic surge through my system. The anxiety rose to a point of unbearable intensity, and I threw the bowl into the sink and took off running. I didn't care where I was going, I just needed to get away from the consuming feeling that was burning through my body.

As I approached the far end of the beach – my outdoor sanctuary – I collapsed in exhaustion. My mother had quietly followed me and caught me in her arms. In that moment, huddled together on the beach, I acknowledged that I had lost my way and couldn't turn the page on my situation, even if I wanted to. This was my first realization that my whole being had been hijacked by a dark and deadly force. I was afraid.

"It's gonna be okay, Jenny dear. It's gonna be okay," my mother said. I clung to the thread of hope in her words as she rocked me like she'd done many years prior.

What started off as a grand achievement in self-discipline had turned into a death trap. I began to question whether skinny was worth the cost. For years, I had been managing my suffering through anorexia, exercise addiction and perfectionism.

Redirected Discipline

I spent many years blaming others for my predicament, eventually coming to the conclusion that blame wasn't moving me forward. Once I realized that blaming others was the lowest form of problem solving, I assumed a more successful attitude – one of compassionate self-awareness.

It gradually became clear to me that I was going to die if I didn't change the course of my life, and that I was the only one who could instigate that change. It was my mess, and only I could clean it up. Ironically, I also knew that the focused discipline that had got me into my addicted state was the same quality I would need, in hefty supply, to get me out. Each day, from there on in, I woke up and directed my discipline toward a new focus of reclaiming my life. Day after day, little by little, through determined effort, my life began to transform.

That Healing Rocky Mountain Feeling

One day near the end of my university degree, my older brother asked me how I was going to fulfill my dream of being a teacher in the state I was in. His question shocked me, and frankly pissed me off. It also drove me to do some thinking. Up until that point in my life, I had been consumed in my own suffering. He was right. There was no way I could make a positive impact on anyone's life in the state I was in. Before I could think about contributing to the world, I needed to heal myself and discover who I was truly was.

In deep reflection, something brave inside me spoke up and asked: *if you could do anything at all, what would you do?* The answer that came out was as surprising as my ability to be able to ask myself the question. If I could do anything, I would work out west in the Rocky Mountains, of course. The answer sang out from my heart. I had never been outside of the Maritimes, and had only seen the odd photo of the Rockies. Crazily, I felt called, and I was determined to listen to the inner guidance that I had silenced for so long.

When I received a letter in the mail inviting me to spend the summer at Moraine Lake Lodge (the same stunning vista once featured on the Canadian twenty-dollar bill), I knew it was the first step in leading me out of the dark cloud I had lived under for so many years.

My job, as a hiking guide, was to develop an interpretive hiking service for guests. The opportunity came as a result of my new focus to reclaim my essence.

My sister Lisa and I drove across the country together. It was a beautiful trip that gave us time to reconnect after our years apart at separate universities. It was particularly healing, as we shared the brokenness of our teen years. For the first time in a very long time, I cried and cried and cried. And then, we laughed and laughed and laughed. As we drove up the winding road toward Moraine Lake Lodge, I peered up with a gaping jaw at the peaks of the most magnificent mountains I had ever encountered. I knew that a universal wisdom had brought me there to blow my mind with its majesty, and it had succeeded.

That summer, I guided visitors from all over the world through pristine alpine trails. Each morning, my fellow pilgrims and I would hike up switchbacks through an evergreen forest, eventually emerging above the tree line. I discovered a beautiful symbolism in my treks, as just two months prior, I was wrestling with the shadow of life-threatening patterns. There I now was, up in the peaks of mountains, gazing out over spectacular views that often brought tears of awe and wonder to my eyes. I returned to my early childhood of being immersed in the natural world, and my whole being began to align with the vibrant essence of Mother Nature. The experience reminded me of the important role that nature played in my healing. My senses began to awaken from their deep slumber, as I listened to the musical and uplifting sounds of the forest, and the fragrance of sap and damp moss filled my nostrils. The fresh mountain air expanded my lungs like opening the windows of a cottage that had been closed for many seasons.

Being immersed in the natural environment helped revive my sense of spontaneity, adventure and play. My colleagues and I would sleep out under the stars, gazing up at the peaks in the moonlight. We cycled through Banff on tandem bikes and did cartwheels on the top of the Tower of Babel. I was beginning to reconnect with the child inside of myself – one who felt loved, whole and safe in the world. Happiness and contentment were finding their way back into my soul.

Over time, I noticed the healthy me was starting to speak in a stronger, more confident voice. It was occurring naturally, as a byproduct of being away from the birthplace of my scars, and through my being of service to others. I also noticed that my body's natural rhythms for sleep, food and rest were re-establishing themselves. My microscopic mindset that obsessed about fear of failure and perfectionism began to dissolve, as I slowly but surely shifted from self-distain to seeing the spark of the divine alive within me.

I yearned to feel beautiful on the inside and be a living example of beauty in the world, in a flowing, glowing and vibrant kind of way – not in a perfect, skinny, runway model kind of way. The natural beauty of my majestic surroundings was helping me to claim that within myself. If nature alone could create a masterpiece such as these mountains, then maybe, just maybe, I was a part of that design.

Clarity of Purpose

Despite the successful teaching and coaching career I went on to build in Vancouver, there remained an emptiness within me that continued to beg for my attention. As I began to dabble in yoga, I found myself drawn to the root of the practice, and I wanted to fully experience the mysterious wisdom presence that seemed to exist beyond the postures. I was hungry to discover who the real me was – the me that lay trapped within the pain of my body obsession and addiction to perfection. Although I was functionally in the world, true happiness eluded me. I was ready to piece the broken parts of myself back together, and the practice of joining my mind with my body through breath seemed like the remedy I needed to heal my soul.

Beyond all logic, I was called to a place far away, in search of finding oneness with myself and the world that I had felt so alienated from. This place was what some call the 'Mother Land,' known to others as India. My first trip there was my first real step toward wholeness. As I purged generations of painful patterns and beliefs, the tangled ball of tension in my body began to unravel.

The Universe has a way of letting us know the things we need to know when we're ready. It was during my second trip to India that I realized that I had a responsibility to share my light with the world. At the time, I remained a fairly inexperienced traveler, who had lived a rather protected life. The developing world was so foreign to me. It was much like stepping onto another planet.

Over several weeks of living and practicing yoga in the intense heat and crush of humanity in India, I grew more relaxed and familiar with myself and the chaotic pace of life. And in the midst of traffic fumes, as I sat in the back seat of an old rickshaw, I experienced a sacred moment that would change my life forever.

The rickshaw had slowed to yield to traffic (a rare occurrence in India), and my eyes scanned a community of people who lived beneath tarps and survived by selling watermelons along the roadside. An older woman caught my eye, and we shared a focused connection for several seconds, as her intense gaze saw directly into my soul. It was as if she was speaking out loud and clearly saying, "Go do something with your life, for yourself and for all of us. We are confined here, but you are not. Go make a difference!" The rickshaw lurched forward into the flow of traffic and our beautiful moment of synchronicity had passed...but was not forgotten.

I knew the connection I shared with that woman was intended as a message to me, and I was both deeply moved and utterly terrified. Heeding the message meant I would have to hurdle the limiting beliefs that kept me small, but feeling safe. It meant that I would have to listen to and obey the vision within my heart, and that was scary. Showing up differently in the world is scary, because we don't really know how it's all going to shake down. Will we be accepted? Successful? Happy? But here's the catch: we'll never truly know unless we go for it. I went for it, and I'm so glad I did.

By developing an unwavering sense of self-worth, I began to ride the waves of life with more grace, skill and optimism. When I dropped the *shoulds* and started following my heart, my true path revealed itself.

Glimpses of the Gift

For a long time, I lamented about not having the self-awareness to identify that I was off track. It would have saved me from so many years of struggle. I now view my time of starvation and isolation as my shamanic journey, or my forty days in the dessert, through which I was exposed to the rawness of the human condition. By being "boiled down to the bones," as they say in AA, I was given the opportunity to recreate myself into a self-loving person with a deep reverence for life. Just like the phoenix – the mythical bird who chose her own death, only to rise radiantly out of her own ashes – who I am today is much stronger than who I ever would have been without my struggle. The gifts of expertise and wisdom that I share with the world through my teaching and writing are a direct result of the hits of pain I endured.

After many years of suffering, and many moments on the brink of giving up, I have emerged from the wreckage of my perfect storm. The life I lead today didn't just fall into place though. With the same focus as an Olympian would approach the podium, I took on the healing process with fierce determination … with the memory of my connection with the woman in India continuing to ignite my flame along the way. Not only was I doing the work for my own benefit, but for the sake of all women everywhere – past, present and future.

My healing came through the process of deeply excavating my dysfunctional behavioral patterns, which go back many generations. Through the work of putting the proverbial stick in the spokes, I not only gained greater understanding of mental illness, but also deep compassion for it. Through body-mind therapies, eastern healing practices and rigorous personal inquiry, I have healed my broken wings and in the process, gained many powerful tools that I now share with others. Today, I fully embrace the gifts in a life filled with career success, fulfilling relationships and vibrant wellbeing. My strong and capable phoenix wings allow me to wake up each morning, excited by the adventure of life, feeling ready to explore new territory. I am infinitely challenged and rewarded daily in my role as mother of two amazing girls, and in my intimate relationship with my beautiful husband and business partner, Blair. Ours is a bond grounded in love, trust and humor.

Professionally, by getting out of my own way and following my hearts calling, I have been able to positively contribute to the lives of hundreds of thousands of people. As founder *Breathing Space Yoga Studios* – a system of licensed businesses – we are dedicated to *Awakening the Extraordinary*. I am a published author of eight *Yoga in Schools* programs – a movement that is spreading into schools across North America. One of the programs is the popular *Yoga Grade 11*, offered as a Physical Education elective. My latest labor of love is the new *Girl on Fire* empowerment program, which celebrates my journey from the ashes and is designed with the intention of helping others avoid the same perfect storm I endured by their living more skillfully and compassionately.

What's most rewarding about my work (which is more fun than work) is the constant feedback we receive almost daily, from schoolteachers and students alike, remarking how yoga has changed, and even saved, their lives. A few years ago, I presented *Yoga in Schools* to three-hundred school teachers in my former high school gymnasium – the exact spot where the perfect storm had once enveloped my life. It was a beautiful moment of recognition of the gift that had blossomed out of the devastation of my teen years.

In the beginning, a seed only needs an ounce of nourishment to grow. That nourishment may come in the form of curiosity, hope, or even despair. It doesn't matter what fuels your journey, so long as you take it. Have patience, relax your expectations, and be willing to leave the past behind you and grow. While healing can be slow and mucky, it can also be instantaneous. Through my own journey of healing, I've discovered that anything is possible when we open our hearts.

A few weeks ago I was cuddling with my girls at bedtime. As I held them each in one arm, I became overwhelmed with love and spontaneously remarked, "Oh what an awesome moment! I wish I had known as a troubled teen, the joy and love that was waiting here for me."

No matter who you are or what struggles you face today, know that the same joy and love await you as you unravel the gifts within your hits.

About Jenny

BIO:

Jenny Kierstead is the founder of national award-winning Breathing Space Yoga Studios and Yoga in Schools. Jenny designed a Yoga Grade 11 course for the Nova Scotia Department of Education, the first ever yoga program implemented in Canadian public schools which is currently offered in most high schools in Atlantic Canada. To support this successful school-based initiative, Jenny and her husband Blair run a highly reputed Yoga Teacher Training Program, incorporating their Yoga for Special Needs Program, Yoga for Autism Program and others. Their latest projects; *Girl on Fire* empowerment program and *Mindfulness in the Classroom* are changing the way teens relate to themselves and others. Jenny is also a yoga trainer for Olympic athletes in Nova Scotia.

As a dedicated student of spiritual wisdom, Jenny's captivating teachings are rooted in over 10,000 hours of study. Jenny and Blair enjoy family life in Halifax, Nova Scotia with their two spirited daughters, Sophia and Isabella.

Websites: www.BreathingSpaceYogaStudio.ca
www.YogainSchools.ca

Jenny Kierstead and her daughters Bella and Sophia

Dave Maginley

HIT:

Facing a rare cancer four times and having a near-death experience, David had to live with deadly tumors that could explode with any heighted emotional state.

GIFT:

David's experience with cancer fueled his awareness of the gift of life. It also led to explorations in the nature of consciousness and how life continues after death. This transformed the quality of his presence with himself, and in his work as a chaplain at a major hospital, where he guides those on the edge of immortality.

A Glimpse of
the Other Side
—DAVID MAGINLEY

I am a newborn giraffe. At least, that's how it feels to be 6'8". I didn't exactly move gracefully through life. Most would have guessed I was destined to be a basketball star, but as an insecure introvert, I preferred the solitude of photography to the competition or company of others. Through the lens, I explored the energy and harmony of nature, and the sense of balance and composition both around me and within me. I was in the initial stages of sensing the spirituality in all things, though I had no understanding of what this would mean in my life ahead.

Living with my father and brother in a struggling town, I knew options after high school were bleak, so I headed to a thriving university city out west to live with my mother, her new husband, and a household of six other children wildly different from me.

One morning, just as I was adapting to my new home, I awoke to find myself bleeding internally. I could see the blood in my urine, though I felt no other side effects. My mother and I rushed to the hospital, where the doctors quickly found a tumor in my bladder. It turned out to be a rare cancer called pheochromocytoma. Typically a benign tumor, mine was life-threatening as it produced a massive amount of hormones, triggered by the release of adrenaline. If I became excited in any way, it could kill me. Fortunately, we caught the tumor early, just as it started to spread into my bladder.

From the moment of diagnosis, my life felt completely different. I remember thinking: *Is this cancer? Am I going to make it?* Yet, I went into surgery feeling perfectly calm. Somehow I knew I'd survive, and sure enough, I did. As I lay there, a seventeen-year-old, both naïve and grateful for life, the patient next to me was recovering from an attempted suicide. All I wanted to do was taste my life, and he had wanted to take his away. I realized in that moment how incapable I was to appreciate the psychological pain he must be going through, and reflected on the paradox of how our different lives had been brought together at that time. Our conversation was to be among many seeds planted over the years, to result in my present career as a spiritual counsellor. I do recall how it made me even more hungry for life. I no longer wanted to be the shy recluse. I wanted to take some risks and experience the wider world. So, even in my state of being bandaged up and enduring the pain of recovery from surgery, I negotiated an evening pass to go to a concert in town. I recall the exhilaration of getting in a taxi, soaking in the performance, and drinking in the moments before me. I felt so engaged, and telling no one about my adventure made it all the more exciting.

Another night, I stayed up to watch a movie in hospital, only to find myself rolling on the floor with laughter at a silly commercial. I felt such abandon, such a release, such life flowing through me. As the nurses helped me stagger to bed (stitches and laughter do not mix!), I was filled with profound gratitude for their care. These moments of deep awareness were held in quiet reverence. I was keenly aware of the texture of my life – I would feel the sun on my face, taste my food with new appreciation, and mindfully walk the hospital corridors. I was awake. I was present. Even years later, enjoying the company of friends, I would be filled with an appreciation that I never wanted to have fade.

My fascination with the deeper levels of life had begun to open up, as as did my questions. Reading and late night discussions could only take me so far. Driven by a renewed thirst for knowledge, I decided to enroll in university to study the meaning of life. It wasn't a great career move, and I was never a great student, but I was enjoying the quest. I explored the mysteries of mind, reality and mysticism through philosophy and comparative religions, as I studied with Catholic and Taoist priests, Anglican ministers, Buddhist monks, Rabbis, atheist, and everyone in between. I had no idea where I was going. I never found answers, but my studies were leading to better questions.

When you graduate with a philosophy degree, you wonder where you can go next. I pursued my hobbies, turning them into a freelance video and computer business that, while fun, was not satisfying. A Masters degree seemed the next best step, but in order to explore the mystical realm of life I would need to set a different course. I decided to enroll in seminary. Interestingly, I still didn't consider myself to be religious, though I was involved in a community of Christian friends, and enjoyed wrestling with ideas through our 2:00a.m. coffee-fuelled conversations.

During my internship year, I had to decide if becoming a minister was really what I wanted to do. There were passing thoughts that maybe I'd become a teacher, but I decided to dive in to the direction I before me. I realized that I truly loved being a minister. I loved being a compassionate presence and exploring, from the pulpit, these deep questions and answers. I was truly coming out of my shell. And then, the cancer returned. It had been ten years since my initial hit.

I was giving a talk in hospital chapel when the tumor kicked in. At first, I had thought the woozy feelings and sweating were nothing more than the nerves naturally produced from speaking in public. And then, I passed out. When you are as tall as me, the fall to the floor is not a graceful or gentle one!

It was this second round with cancer that brought me to my near-death experience. Suddenly, I was released from my physical body, and found myself on a green hillside. I could feel the movement of every blade of grass, as I stood alive with wonder and excitement in a place that can only be described as 'home.' I wanted to run to the top of the hill, when I noticed that there was someone by my side. He was profoundly wise and felt like an old friend. This being told me I was doing a good job, but that I couldn't stay in this hillside paradise. There was more work to be done. Despite my protest, he said I had to go back, and before I knew it, I was. Returning to my body was traumatic. I immediately felt like its weight and density were a prison. The poverty of words was so slow compared to the mental communication I had just experienced. Rather than feeling relief, I was consumed with profound sadness. Life is so two-dimensional here, compared with the splendor and heightened consciousness of that other realm.

Those moments on the other side left an indelible impression upon me, but I buried my near-death experience. I didn't talk about it, mostly because of my existential shift from a place of such love and joy back to this one of profound limitation. I dared not tell anyone in the years ahead how I longed to be back in that place.

The doctors did some investigations and found the second tumor in my femoral artery. Unlike my first round of cancer, this time I felt the effects strongly. My tumor was producing a Molotov cocktail of hormones, resulting in heart palpitations, sweating and a horrible physical uneasiness. I had countless episodes of profound stomach cramps, diarrhea and fainting spells. That was when we became aware of how severe my condition truly was, and how many times feeling strong positive or negative emotions placed my life in danger.

Surgery was risky. The tumor was metabolically active and very dangerous, even if less than an inch in diameter. As I headed for the operating room, I secretly wished for another look at the other side – a glimpse of that place I knew to be home. Of course, I never did get it. I did, however, awake with the same intense appreciation of the gift of life. I felt the measure of my days, and I was engaged with the moments before me. That was exhilarating enough.

Life went on, and among its gifts was news that my wife and I were expecting a son. It should have been the greatest gift of all, yet it was bittersweet, as the cancer returned for a third time. This time it was larger and even more active. I had frequent episodes of anxiety, heart palpitations, pain that doubled me over, and passing out without warning. I wondered if I could I even survive my son's birth. Amazingly and miraculously, the profound excitement and joy of his arrival did not activate the tumor. Instead, I was filled with deep peace and gratitude. Holding him, I somehow knew my journey was far from over.

I had accepted a position at a country parish on the wide open Canadian Prairies, in a tiny village with a big heart that treated a rookie minister well. Eventually, we moved back to the east coast, where I was fortunate to continue my explorations in the nature of consciousness through meditation. It had become a vital tool which enabled me to deal with the wild fluctuations in adrenaline that had threatened me with a quick and premature death on so many occasions. The practice of meditation was invaluable, as three years following my third incidence of cancer, a forth tumor was found in my lymph nodes. It was spreading.

It's interesting, even ridiculous, how we try to maintain a normal façade while facing our mortality. Every effort is spent fighting with determination for more moments of life, yet we are not authentically engaged in the moments we have. How much wiser it is to work with the wisdom of grief and contemplating death. Most cultures of the world encourage this, embrace it as part of life. In the west, it becomes, at best, the secret world within the patient. I quietly negotiated with my mortality, smiling all the way through. As much as that was my mask, the peace that once again came upon me during surgery, and in the intensive care during a brief cardiac crisis, affirmed I was supported by angels unseen. The work that I was meant to do, mentioned by my heavenly companion on the hillside paradise, was yet to be revealed.

Back at home, I felt the texture of my life deeply once again, but I was also filled with discontent. Greater questions began to surface. *What do I do with this? Where is my life going?* I knew that I wasn't fully happy as a minister. There was a restlessness growing within me. I wasn't at home in my own life, and somethings needed to shift.

My wife and I divorced, and I moved to half-time at my parish. In what should have been a time of great instability and anxiety, it felt like a new beginning. In a short time, a job opened up as a chaplain at the hospital. This was it, I knew it! That was where I needed to be! Leaving parish ministry, I dove into caring for those with cancer and, not surprisingly, found my heart's deepest calling. As challenging as it was, I found it incredibly exciting, deeply rewarding and a profound privilege. My work brought me back to myself.

That was thirteen years ago. Through the pursuit of my purpose, I have been presented with choices – choices about career, relationships, how to be a father, how to care and love my body, and how to be a good steward of life. I discovered through meditation how we can modulate our consciousness, shift our experience, and connect deeply to the here and now – the only place there is. I began exploring how, through compassionate and authentic presence with ourselves, we not only love, but become love itself. Tuning into that launched my life forward. I moved into a healthy, loving relationship and remarried. I began to deeply explore the nature of consciousness, spiritual technologies, and the physics of immortality. My spirituality deepened and matured. I was supporting people at the edge of life, and experiencing frequent mystical moments at work, including patients sharing their own near-death experiences. This resulted in my joining the International Association for Near-Death Studies, contributing to research and presenting workshops on the greatest of puzzles: the nature of consciousness, and whether it continues.

Consciousness is the ultimate mystery. For decades, I had bought into the age old arguments of whether there was a God, or science versus spirituality. The real question to ask is quite different: What is what is the nature of consciousness? It is universally experienced, yet impossible to measure. We see signs of its presence – brain activity, heart beat, body heat – but what it is that manifests 'you' – the being that remains beyond the scope of objective, rational proof?

For years, I had wrestled with how to express this in words and put it all into a book. Procrastination and giving into the thoughts that I could never complete such a project delayed such efforts for years. Then, after a particularly difficult case in which a young mother died, something unlocked within me. I got up at 4:00a.m.and started putting into words what, for so long, felt nearly impossible to describe. Two years later, the first draft of my book was complete. Its message is nothing new: God is love. Our true purpose is not just to love, but to become love, to evolve into love. The expression of that universal message was now truly my own – my voice and the deep wisdom gained from my patients. I have learned from them that we best accomplish this transformation of our being when we engage suffering through compassion. The authentic and integrated heart is not one marked by control, strength and peace, but one able to embrace the brokenness, the unfinished love story, and use it for growth. This is what Jesus did. This is what I was growing into. This is a spirituality which enables us to do more than go through cancer; it empowers us to grow through cancer.

It is very simple and very difficult. It requires strength and vulnerability, a focus on being authentic and aware, a curiosity and trust that love is the bottom line, and courage in your core. By focusing on becoming love, you really are doing the most noble, wisest thing possible. This is the hero's journey, the universal story of all our lives – to use our trials to discover who we truly are: unique expressions of God's consciousness. Feel your mortality, while trusting your immortality. And, as Christian, I realized this meant we are called to believe *into* Christ, not simply believe *in* Christ. It's about becoming one with divine consciousness.

The journey will be unique for each of us. We each experience struggles that challenge us to be authentic and not shrink back from the hard homework of the heart. How we sabotage ourselves! The instinct is to put on a strong face and keep it all together. This is so ironic, as it means that while dealing with cancer and fighting for more moments of life, we tend to avoid the moment we're in! Cancer taught me to have a sense of humor about that, to be compassionate with myself and others, and to engage with my experience and internal world and hold the mess of it all, while manifesting love. There is no need to fix or correct our challenges, as much as to learn to love through them, being in the here and now.

Cancer has brought me to my best self (which still remains inconsistent, as I am human). It taught me to be graceful and forgiving for my imperfections (which are never-ending), and it amplified the gift of life beyond anything I could have imagined.

Providing spiritual care to those facing cancer inevitably takes it toll on you. To maintain a healthy balance, this secondary trauma must be processed, and for me the camera continues to be a powerful therapeutic tool. It is a tool for self-psychology, revealing hidden aspects of my subconscious and the nature of spirit. Through the lens, I continue to learn of myself, becoming more connected to my own brief journey and opening to the shadow aspects of the self, as well as to the light. The camera looks both ways. Photography has brought me back to what I sensed in my youth, training the eye to see that the signature of divine consciousness is everywhere.

With my patients, I'll ask if they have a creative expression – an approach to self-understanding. When words fail us, creativity becomes a more direct path to the material hidden within our hearts. By creating, we are actually participating in the same sacred process as the divine. While the purpose of love is to connect consciousness, the purpose of creativity is to expand consciousness. How staggering to also discover that we see the world as we are, not as the world is. This means everything we feel, say, think and do reveals truth only about ourselves. We become the lens through which the image is focused. We also become the projector, creating our reality in partnership with all others, collectively building on the experience of the universe. And, what we create will be eternal, when focused on love.

At seventeen, when the cancer first hit, I could never imagine what would unfold. Without it, I know I would be a far different man. The gift of my hit was the ultimate lesson that love is the only thing that's real and eternal, because God is love. Anything I create, believe, manifest that is not of love, simply will not last. Jesus knew that, manifested that, and taught that. As I remember that, I live of life of much deeper forgiveness, and am able to treat myself with a bit more compassion and a much larger sense of humor! In this way, cancer brought me into myself. It was and is a great teacher.

Even having been in remission for thirteen years now, I wouldn't be surprised if the cancer comes back. If it does it does, if it doesn't it doesn't. Ours isn't always a happy ending. We can't be shielded from suffering, we can only step into it and use it to grow.

I do feel that I am full steam ahead on the work I am suppose to do. Even though I'm home sick for the other side, I don't want to die just yet. I have an amazing life, a book to publish, more work to do, and more love to grow into. The wonder of exploring our spiritual nature, and the privilege of supporting those who will soon find out, leaves me filled with gratitude for the hit.

About David

BIO:

David Maginley is the interfaith chaplain for the cancer program, palliative care and intensive care at the QEII Health Sciences Centre in Halifax, Nova Scotia, and author of *Beyond Surviving: Cancer and Your Spiritual Journey*. He has survived a rare cancer four times, which led to a profound near-death experience and explorations in consciousness and the connection of body, mind and spirit. With degrees in philosophy, and as an ordained minister, David has a deep sense of purpose in supporting others in their spiritual journey. He knows what it's like to have cancer from both sides of the hospital bed, and to have a sense of this life from both sides of the veil.

David is a certified specialist with the Canadian Association for Spiritual Care, a minister with the Lutheran Church in Canada, and a member of the Canadian Association of Psychosocial Oncology, the Atlantic Therapeutic Touch Network, the Institute of Noetic Sciences, and the International Association for Near-Death Studies. His book, *Beyond Surviving: Cancer and your Spiritual Journey*, will be available soon on Amazon.com.

Website: www.davidmaginley.com

David Maginley

Michael Millette

HIT:

Michael and Jackie's lives changed dramatically after Jackie developed the first symptoms of ALS in 2005. The disease took Jackie's life in the fall of 2012.

GIFT:

Through being an intimate witness to unimaginable suffering and heartache, Michael has come to know the true meaning of grace and acceptance, and now carries with him a deep empathy for other people suffering through horrendous illness.

Rising Above
Suffering and Despair
— MICHAEL AND JACKIE

Forever will I remember the day I met Jackie on a mountain trail. I think we might have even sensed right there, in that very first moment, that we were destined to walk the same path and that we had stumbled upon our future in each other by the merest of fortuitous chances. It was a powerful feeling. Jackie was exciting, beautiful, intelligent, and a lot of fun.

As we began sharing more time together, we could see how we complemented each other in so many ways. Jackie brought discipline and common sense into my world, and I contributed my resourcefulness to hers. It was a synergistic relationship. We accomplished so much more as a couple than either of us could possibly have hoped for on our own.

Together, we decided to start buying and selling properties, in particular, homes that needed a lot of work. The experience I had gained through years as an industrial and construction electrician and general handyman served us well in our renovation projects. Before we met, Jackie had spent a good part of her adult life travelling the world, working on farms, practicing massage, learning yoga and mountain climbing. Home renovations had not been on her list of skills, though nothing daunted her.

Our life was easy and comfortable. It simply felt right. Neither of us questioned the fact that we had found our soul mate. It was for the most part, an effortless slide into a full-on life commitment. We took care of each other, leading a full, active and productive life. Focus and hard work were the cornerstones of our values, allowing us to get a whole lot accomplished. We were *weapons of mass production*. But still, in the midst of all the work, we found the time to go hiking and take extended overseas holidays. Though we practiced frugality and financial common sense, spending money on things we deemed important was never a problem. We were obviously doing something right, because all of a sudden, we found ourselves in financial abundance.

Having a passion for parachuting and snowboarding, I bought myself a brand new parachute and snowboarding gear. Together, Jackie and I took flying lessons and bought ourselves a little airplane. We also bought a Roland Fantom keyboard so that Jackie could accompany my guitar playing. Having never before known such financial freedom, I even bought a motorcycle. It seemed as though nothing was out of reach, and our bank account just seemed to keep growing without much effort on our part.

After five short years and seven home renovation projects, we had built our equity to well over $600,000. At that rate we would be millionaires within a few short years. It felt good not to have to worry about money anymore, though we also were keenly aware that there was a lot more to life than money. We intuitively understood the law of universal abundance in which money played only a small part. Life was meant to be experienced. The world was meant to be explored. We were meant to be self-actualized, to be the best we could be. And, above all, we were meant to love and be loved. These were the things that really mattered, and these were the things that we pursued. We even kept a little calendar record of our physical intimacy. There were very few days on that calendar, even after five years, that didn't have a little red heart colored in. Some days had two or three hearts. We played music and did yoga together. It really did feel as if we were living life to the absolute fullest. I loved her more than I ever imagined was possible.

Jackie decided to start a weekly routine of playing indoor soccer with some friends. One evening she came home disappointed in herself, saying she had been particularly clumsy with the ball. Over the course of the next few days, it became apparent that there was something going on with her right foot. She wasn't quite limping, but nor was she able to run properly. We figured that she had tweaked or twisted something. We both just assumed that it was a minor injury that would get better in a week or two.

Strangely, Jackie's injury seemed to grow worse as the days passed. A couple of weeks later, she was visibly limping. Jackie's focus and drive shifted gears. She starting spending time on the internet, researching muscle and nerve damage. All the while, her limping continued to worsen. She began to feel panicked and anxious. Walking into the kitchen one evening, she caught her reflection in the glass of the back sliding doors and realized just how bad her limp had gotten. She was determined to figure out what was happening.

I remember watching Jackie climb down some scaffolding we had set up to install a new window one day and limp awkwardly across the grass, on her way back inside the house. Through the window, I watched her across the bedroom floor, toward me. We puckered and kissed through the glass. It is a poignant memory of seeing my beautiful Jackie, my healthy and vibrant and strong, mountain-climbing Jackie, struggling so. It has become both a sad and a happy memory. She was so determined, so disciplined, so strong. It all seemed so unfair.

Jackie's condition continued to worsen, though slowly. Several doctors, including two Neurologists, were either reluctant or unable to give her a diagnosis. Eventually, she was referred to a Neurologist at a Vancouver hospital that specialized in nervous system disorders. The testing was painful. Long thin needles wired to a monitoring machine, were pushed deeply into the flesh of her thighs. Dr. Briemberg studied the machine readout, faced us both, and in a calm matter of fact tone, announced that she had ALS. She told us that Jackie could expect to live, at the most, five more years.

ALS is a neurological disorder in which a person slowly, but steadily, loses motor control of the entire body. The mechanism or cause of failure in the motor neurons is essentially unknown. There is no cure, and there are no effective treatments. Dr. Briemberg suggested that we make a series of appointments with various specialists. There was nothing they could do to prolong her life, though they did offer to put her on a program that would help us cope. We never did return to that hospital. That diagnosis could have been her worst fears confirmed, but it wasn't. Jackie never accepted that ALS was going to rule her life.

Our first order of business was clearing everything else off our plate, so we could focus on the task at hand: Jackie's health. We found a newly constructed comfortable rancher, settled in and got right down to the business of fixing what we saw as the temporary little glitch that was going on in her body. I knew from the very first day I met Jackie that she was an extraordinary woman, but the measure of a truly extraordinary person never becomes fully apparent until it is tested.

Jackie taught me many things, challenging and changing my personal perspective, and consequently, my approach to life. Nobody wants to die prematurely. Nobody wants a debilitating and horrible disease like ALS, but when it does strike, most will give in to the belief that they have a fatal illness. Jackie was not like most people. Some might consider her belief misguided or unrealistic, but to me, her approach showed a strength of will and character that was truly inspiring. I couldn't help but feel excited with the prospect of helping her to turn this thing around. If our life up to this point could be used as an indication of what was possible, then we would be climbing mountains again before too long.

There was no way that either of us could possibly have known what lay ahead.

From a purely objective perspective, ALS is a truly confounding disease that presents in a variety of ways. Some people only live a year; and in some rare cases, others live as long as twenty or even thirty years after diagnosis. Interestingly, our research revealed that there was a high incidence of cases amongst the American military who had served in the Gulf War, and that there are less people with ALS per capita in tropical countries. It also tends to affect more men than women, and mostly those older than fifty. Lyme disease has been known to mimic the symptoms of ALS, as has heavy metal toxicity. We also know that about five per cent of all ALS cases can be linked to genetic inheritance.

Jackie chose to consider her affliction more as a set of symptoms or a syndrome, rather than as a labeled disease. She held firm to the belief that the body is capable of healing itself from any illness, or disorder, and that every disease has a cure… and most often a simple one. In her mind, it was just a matter of time before the cure was discovered. This belief resonated with me as well. It just made sense. There was no shortage of information on the internet, even if much of it was ambiguous or out-right contradictory.

We buckled down and began to sort through it all. One of our first steps was to fly to the Dominican Republic for a stem cell injection. Six months later, we found ourselves in a hospital in the heart of southern China, where they specialized in offering traditional Chinese medicine to Western and European people. Chinese medicine has a different understanding and approach to working with the body's nervous system, though it has proved to be no more effective than traditional western medicine in dealing with the complexities of ALS.

Six months after the treatments in China, we found ourselves at the Bandon Hyperbaric Oxygen Chamber Clinic in Ireland. The clinic was run by volunteers and available to anyone with a need. The price was $10 per session – a mere fraction of what it would ordinarily cost. By that time, Jackie had lost much of her leg function, but she could still hobble around with the use of a cane. Sometimes though, it just made more sense for me to piggyback her, particularly so as we set out to explore the rest of Ireland. The castle ruins were not equipped with elevators.

Our next healing adventure was an extended seven-month trip, which included three months in a Lyme treatment clinic in Reno, Nevada. I became Jackie's legs, piggybacking her everywhere. I suppose we could have gotten a wheelchair, but it just didn't seem necessary. I think we both felt a degree of comfort in her clinging tightly around my neck and shoulders. People would stare and wonder, and sometimes ask ques-tions. Jackie had learned to depend on me, and I felt privileged to be depended on.

The nerve deterioration in Jackie's body was steadily progressing, though gradually. It was perceptible only over a period of several months. She never gave up on herself, and she continued to inspire me to not give up on her either. She found a blood treatment clinic in Tijuana, Mexico, and it was time to hit the road again. We spent several months in a Best Western motel in San Diego, just across the border. We became a part of a large community of people in that motel who were also visiting Mexican clinics. There is a real camaraderie, a common bond, amongst people who have known suffering through illness.

Our next stop, accompanied by our two caregivers, was San Juan, Puerto Rico. The doctor there had stumbled upon a truly extraordinary treatment program for restoring a damaged nervous system. We witnessed first-hand, dramatic real improvement in people with various degrees of paralysis. We had good reason to feel hopeful. Sadly, the mechanism of failure in Jackie's nervous system couldn't be managed as easily as repairing a nerve damaged through trauma.

After a few years of focused effort, Jackie's body was still failing her; however, not for one moment did she give up. We continued to research, she remained determined, and the strength of her will and spirit continued to shine through. Our efforts persisted, as we visited a few other clinics and purchased an enormous amount of specialized equipment for use at home. Jackie also had a port-o-cath surgically implanted in order to facilitate heavy metal detoxification at home through chelation protocols. She was willing to try anything.

Life had become more than a little unusual. Our front door was never locked. There must have been at least twenty caregivers and friends who became accustomed to just walking right in. It felt very much like having a really large, loving, close-knit family. Gone was our precious solitary, independent life. While much of the quiet and peace we once knew had disappeared, both Jackie and I welcomed these wonderful people into our world, and into our hearts. It was them who made life bearable, more comfortable and possible. They sat with us during the heartaches and the challenges, and as a consequence of their direct involvement, there were a lot of happy, uplifting moments during a very trying time.

While our private life may have been a thing of the past, that didn't mean that physical intimacy was no longer important. Living with ALS meant being creative and continuously adapting to new situations. It meant seizing any opportunity to stretch out beside Jackie and hold her hand or stroke her hair. If anything, our feelings for each other deepened during this time.

Continuing with our traditions and practices was what kept us going, and Jackie's determination to do so was incredible. She refused to acknowledge the fact that she could no longer stand, as she used custom made leg braces and a therapy walker to help her get vertical. She also didn't ever stop doing yoga; she just altered the way she did her practice, employing other people to move her limbs.

For three years, we had a team of hard-working caregivers with us for thirteen hours a day, doing extensive body work and helping with various healing protocols. We bought a deep therapy hot tub where we spent an hour and a half pretty much every single day, just before bed time. That session would help calm Jackie's twitching muscles and aid her in getting to sleep. We came to truly value our hot tub time, as it helped us to cope. Sometimes, we sat there in silence together and sometimes we commiserated or talked about the bizarre nature of life. Sometimes Jackie would speak about her deepest fears, while I took notes on the computer. Sometimes we just cuddled. Always, we watched an episode or two of some HBO television series on the computer. It was a special time of day for us … a happy little ritual.

ALS is emotionally challenging for everyone involved. It is a real life horror story of epic proportions. Coping can be a huge struggle, but I managed to find a couple of very effective distractions. Writing about the experience helped me to make some sense out of what was happening. Playing my guitar proved to really help as well. I got together with a few friends and formed a classic rock cover band called the Earthlings. We would jam in our garage at night, as Jackie and her caregiver listened from inside the house. Fortunately, our neighbours were just as appreciative.

Jackie suffered with ALS for over eight years before it worked its way into her mouth and throat, and eventually took her life. There were a lot of dark moments in those years, filled with emotional and physical suffering. The experience, all in all, was anything but enjoyable. I think that I can say in truth that I wish it didn't happen; but it did, and that simple fact can never change.

Despite the pain and in spite of the horror, in the midst of the suffering, there were powerful life-changing lessons that shined through. Jackie learned grace and acceptance. She learned how to let go of the ego, and even though, at first glance, it might seem like a hit one could do without, she came to be completely and truly at peace with what happened. My own spirituality evolved through the experience as well, as it opened me to acceptance and a deep-rooted feeling of genuine calm and peace.

Having loved such a woman as Jackie, to have been such an integral part of her life was a privilege that I will forever be grateful for. It was an extraordinary privilege to love her and stand witness to her beauty, courage and grace after diagnosis and through the progression of the disease. The experience has impacted me profoundly. Along with Jackie, I suffered emotionally far beyond what anybody should reasonably be expected to in a single lifetime.

Fear and uncertainty are fundamental and familiar feelings within all of us. As a result of this hardship, my fear and uncertainty were replaced with love and understanding. I developed a sincere empathetic love for those among us whose lives are punctuated with profound suffering. I have come to understand or accept what the first tenet of Buddhism teaches us: "Life is suffering." It is through this suffering that the most noble of goals, the shedding of our ego, becomes possible. My *gift of the hit* was born out of the fires of suffering and despair…though it remains an ongoing journey.

When approached by Peter Davison with a request that I contribute a chapter to this compilation book, I replied with enthusiasm and an honest conviction that I really was a better man for having lived through such a horrific experience as watching my best friend and lover fade away through the ravages of ALS. Peter suggested that I might have something of importance to say within a book that sought to reveal the silver lining within the darkest of storm clouds. At the time, I had thought this would be an easy task, and perhaps even a cathartic process. As it turned out, I struggled with identifying the gift within my hit.

I attributed my difficulty with writing something uplifting to the fact that Jackie's death was still very recent. If felt only natural that my grief and emotions would mask, or at least minimize, any positive aspects of my experience. Regardless, I conjured up a plausible gift – a realistic sort of self-actualizing transformation that was tinged with an element of truth and would ultimately be realized…something that would develop in time. Of course, there are some very real, tangible positive changes that I could easily identify. I have learned true compassion and empathy, and I understand what it means to honour and respect life. I have spent many hours in silent contemplation these past few years, and can honestly say I have come to terms with my own mortality through becoming more aware of the bigger picture.

The transformation is not yet complete, however. Many of the changes I had anticipated have not yet happened. I fear that maybe they will never happen. Perhaps I need to re-evaluate my *gift of the hit*. Perhaps though, it is nothing to fear at all. Perhaps it is more about coming to terms with feelings and emotions and accepting that my gift is something more sublime. As I contemplate life and identify what might legitimately be considered a positive consequence of the tragedy that I was a part of for so many years, I will admit to feeling a form of calm inner peace.

I never did subscribe to the notion that whatever doesn't kill you makes you stronger, and this experience only reinforces this feeling. I don't need to feel stronger. That is not so very important as it turns out. What is important, is that calm peaceful acceptance after the storm, and the honest understanding that even though we may not know all the answers or the reasons why things happen, that they are exactly as they are meant to be. I will be alright. I am alright. Although, never does a day go by that I don't miss Jackie terribly. She was both my gift and the source of the greatest hit of my life. The process of seeing beyond the storm cloud, I suppose, will simply take time. Whether the revelation comes in the form of slight glimmerings of hope or the skies being awash with a rebirthing powerful light, I have full confidence that the full gift of being witness to such pain and suffering will finally become clear.

About Michael

BIO:

After leaving the small Ontario town where he grew up, Michael forged a new life in northern British Columbia. Those were important formative years, as he became an industrial electrician and raised a family. His adventurous spirit is reflected in his passion for snowboarding, skydiving, mountain climbing and experiencing the world through travel – activities that have remained a constant in his ever-changing life.

He met and had five great years with Jackie, before she became sick and their lives changed direction. Healing from her tragic suffering and loss, Michael wrote their story in a memoire titled *A Hope in Hell*. Also a tender and heart-felt musician, Michael has crafted multiple songs that speak to both the profound and simple aspects of life.

Today, Michael has created a comfortable life teaching at a technical school in the Middle East. He plans to settle down on the east coast of Canada to be a part of his grandchildren's lives as they grow up.

Jackie and Michael

Epilogue

Our unique hits come in different shapes, sizes and timing. In any case, the shock of news, change or adversity that forever shifts the course of our lives can be difficult to process. Healing is a journey that unfolds in unique timing for all of us. The realization of any gifts tucked beneath the surface of our hits happens when we are ready to see and embrace them. For some, the hit can linger in a fog of pain and grief for some time. For others, clarity begins to emerge more quickly. There is no right or wrong, or rhyme or reason, as to how we absorb and work through the adversities of our lives. It is personal, and it is a choice.

Despite this section being called the epilogue, there truly is no final word to a book like this. Much like each of the contributing authors, we all will continue to grow and confront the highs and lows of life. We will continue to forget, and we will remember. The biggest thing we can do, and greatest gift we have to draw from within, is to be more conscious of our choices and perspectives.

For now, we hope that at least one of the stories shared within this book resonated on a similar wavelength to what you are feeling or facing in your life, creating hope for your today and tomorrows. If you felt inspired to boldly take action, to change your circumstance or outlook, to see the world differently, or to see someone going through a hard time more compassionately, then the book has succeeded in its intention.

We encourage you to lend your personal story or that of someone who has inspired you with their journey to an upcoming version of the *Gift of the Hit* Series. There are many more books to come, so please check out the different theme categories at the www.giftofthehit.com. As a special bonus, people who read this are encouraged to visit our resources page to gain access to both free and priced resources to support the unwrapping of the gifts within your hits. www.giftofthehit.com/resources.com.

From here, the gift continues....

CPSIA information can be obtained
at www.ICGtesting.com
Printed in the USA
LVOW12s0506030916
502801LV00004B/4/P